P9-APD-803

Cultural Critique and Abstraction

Cultural Critique and Abstraction

Marianne Moore and the Avant-garde

Elisabeth W. Joyce

Lewisburg
Bucknell University Press
London: Associated University Presses

Associated University Presses
440 Forsgate Drive
Cranbury, NJ 08512

Associated University Presses
16 Barter Street
London WC1A 2AH, England

Associated University Presses
P.O. Box 338, Port Credit
Mississauga, Ontario
Canada L5G 4L8

The paper used in this publication meets the requirements
of the American National Standard for Permanence of Paper
for Printed Library Materials Z39.48–1984.

Library of Congress Cataloging-in-Publication Data

Joyce, Elisabeth W., 1957–
Cultural critique and abstraction : Marianne Moore and the avant-garde / Elisabeth W. Joyce.
p. cm.
Includes bibliographical references (p.) and index.
ISBN 0-8387-5371-X (alk. paper)
1. Moore, Marianne, 1887–1972—Criticism and interpretation. 2. Women and literature—United States—History—20th century. 3. Avant-garde (Aesthetics)—United States—History—20th century. 4. Abstraction in literature. 5. Culture in literature. I. Title.
PS3525.05616Z685 1998
811'.52—dc21 97-41274
CIP

PRINTED IN THE UNITED STATES OF AMERICA

Contents

Acknowledgments

A very early stage of this book was my doctoral dissertation. I would like to thank Susan Stewart, Rachel Blau DuPlessis, and Robert Storey for their continual support of this project and for finally teaching me how to write. I would also like to thank the various people who read later sections and offered much needed advice: Cristanne Miller, Evelyn Hinz, and Cynthia Hogue. Without the kindness and generosity of the staffs at the Rosenbach Museum and Library and the Edinboro University of Pennsylvania Library, this book could never have been written. Also, the warm interest of the Marianne Moore Society has made me understand the place of this work in the field. Finally, I would like to thank those who never lost faith in me during this project: Elise Schiller, Joseph Tabbi, Bruce Joyce, Elizabeth Joyce, and Britton Chance, and all the members of the Thin Books Club. I hereby dedicate this book to my family, to James, Cyrus, and Ursula Parlin, who mean the world to me.

I thank authors, publishers, and other copyright holders for permission to reproduce copyright materials as follows:

Excerpts from *The Complete Poems of Marianne Moore* © 1986 by Lawrence E. Brinn and Louise Crane, executors of the estate of Marianne Moore, are reprinted by permission of Simon and Shuster, Faber and Faber, and the estate of Marianne Moore.

Excerpts from *Observations* © 1924 by Marianne Moore are reprinted by permission of Faber and Faber.

Excerpts from "Sea Rose" by H. D. are reprinted by permission of New Directions Press.

Unpublished materials by Marianne Moore are reprinted with permission from the Rosenbach Museum and Library and the estate of Marianne Moore.

A version of the essay on "Marriage" appeared in *Mosaic* and is reprinted here with that journal's permission.

List of Abbreviations

O   *Observations* (New York: The Dial Press, 1924)

CP   *The Complete Poems of Marianne Moore* (New York: Macmillan, 1967)

Introduction

At a conference run by the National Poetry Foundation in Maine last year, I represented myself to other participants as a scholar of the poetry of Marianne Moore. The reception of this news was remarkable to me because, as a whole, professional teachers of poetry told me that they found her work extremely difficult to understand, much less to teach. What struck me the most about this response was that these very professors had no trouble teaching the equally "difficult" work of other modernist poets, that of Ezra Pound, T. S. Eliot, William Carlos Williams, Wallace Stevens, and Gertrude Stein. The question of what has given Moore the reputation of writing particularly arcane ("intelligent," one of these literary critics described it in awe) poetry in an era during which poetry was especially abstract has driven much of the work of this book. Why is it, I keep asking myself, that Moore's poetry is received with such trepidation, as if it were separate from her contemporaries' work? The answer, I believe, is in the sharp division between her private and public personae and in the paradoxical way that her poetry represents not how Moore wanted herself to be perceived but the reclusive sphere of her life. Her poetry appears, therefore, to be more elusive and resistant to elucidation than it really is because it is so deeply invested in subversion, but a subversion that Moore felt compelled to mask.

In some ways Moore is responsible for subverting her own reputation as a poet through her public persona, however, and in so doing, disrupting reception of her poetry. Moore created a public image that transgressed the intellectual and avant-garde models for the artist in a way that made her lose serious critical attention. She wrote popular and occasional poems later in her life and embarked upon publicity stunts, such as appearing on the June 1966 cover of *Esquire* magazine and in

1968 throwing out the first baseball of the season for the Yankees. Charles Molesworth, in his biography of Marianne Moore, says that the public identified Moore with baseball, and that articles by George Plimpton about Moore's interest in sports, especially boxing and baseball, appeared in not only *Harpers* but *Sports Illustrated* .[1] As much as the avant-gardists pretended to be invested in social and political issues, they were yet scornful of popular culture and so dismissed Moore's poetry as the production of one who could not possibly deserve to be ranked as an artistic equal.

Moore enhanced her distance from her own work by her modesty and demureness about it. In interviews, she often dismisses the value of her work or the effort required to produce it.[2] As I note later in this book, she brushed off Grace Schulman's query about possibly her most serious and most ambitious poem, "Marriage," by saying that it was simply the result of gathering together materials and quotations at hand, as she says, "an anthology of words."[3] By expressing her own assessment of her poetry as a trivial task, Moore undervalues it, and in doing so, deflects serious attention from it.

In the past few years, however, criticism has begun to redress this misapprehension of Moore's poetry, but in an interestingly binary manner, calling attention to and driving a distinction between her conventional personal life and her renegade poetic style. Betsy Erkkila calls Moore a "modernist anomaly"; Cynthia Hogue refers to her "radical conservatism" and describes her as "a New Woman who observed a Victorian standard of decorum in her life, an avant-garde poet whose writing practice is informed by an earlier feminism's ethos of service."[4] There is something about the way that Moore lived and behaved, so quietly, so staidly, so, as Hogue puts it, "decorously," that has confuted critical response of her work. How is it possible that a woman who was so modest and conformist in her personal life could be so radical, so innovative, so culturally critical in her poetry, a poetry that seems to take on established traditions and beliefs in order to argue the need to reshape them into less stifling ones? Erkkila and Hogue, as well as many other critics working right now, move on to admit Moore into the pantheon of modernist poets, but the attention to her dress and to her public persona indicates the still-present deflection of attention from her work, in addition to the puzzlement as to how she was dismissed for so long from this canon.[5]

The truth, which many critics are reinforcing, is that Marianne Moore was an avant-garde artist and was living in and actively involved in New York City at a time when the American art scene was coming into its own. Linda Leavell and Lisa M. Steinman, for instance, have done extensive work to place Moore in the artistic and cultural center of early twentieth-century America, particularly in the world of the visual arts.[6] Steinman notes Moore's "understanding of how the New York art community could provide a context—a sense of power" for the developing poet.[7] New York was at that moment uprooting the Europeans from their central position in the arts. The first and second world wars sent many expatriate artists to this city, and native American artists were drawn there as well, to this environment that accepted, developed, and produced artists who embraced movements such as dadaism and cubism and artistic techniques such as collage and photomontage.

It would, in fact, have been impossible for Moore's poetry to have escaped being influenced by these vigorous upheavals in the arts. Jacques Derrida's reading of Immanuel Kant's theory of the *parergon* proves this point, that any artistic production is permeated by its context, by all aspects of its social conditions. The issue that Derrida and Kant are addressing is at what point the work of art ends and at what point all that is exterior to it begins. Derrida is intrigued by this topic because he is looking for "the true, full originary meaning" of the work.[8] The problem that he faces is that the frame of a work, that which delineates it from its surroundings, is not fixed or solid; it is permeable and it shifts ground; it "merges into the wall, and then, gradually into the general text. . . . [T]he *parergon* is a form which has as its traditional determination not that it stands out but that it disappears, buries itself, effaces itself, melts away at the moment it deploys its greatest energy."[9]

The *parergon* draws what is outside a painting (or, I would argue, a poem) into the work's interior so that the outside becomes an integral part of the inside of the work, or, the reverse, it draws what is inside the work into what is external to it. One of Derrida's metaphors for this action on the part of the frame is "invagination," the folding in of outside material so that it has the quality of the interior. He sees the frame as no more solid than the membrane of a cell, allowing, even encouraging, passage through it both inwardly and outwardly, so that the work of art becomes tainted with what is, according to the frame, outside of it, and so that the work at the same time taints what is around it. There is a constant leakage in both directions.

In accordance with theories such as that posed by Derrida on the *parergon*, recent critics of Marianne Moore's poetry are realizing that her work was deeply influenced by its social and historical context. They are understanding poetry's role in its culture, in general, and sensing the impossibility that Moore could have escaped this role. Cristanne Miller asserts Moore's interest in gender and race issues in *Marianne Moore: Questions of Authority*; Carolyn Burke argues that "the cultural 'composition' of a given society is reflected in the formal structures of its literary 'compositions'"; Jeanne Heuving uses the theories of Pierre Macheray to contend that "all meanings are born out of social tensions."[10]

Each of these critics is suggesting that poetry is engaged in its engendering culture. Culture, however, is not some immutable, monstrous entity—it is in a continual state of flux. Cultural change is ponderous and normally scarcely visible, but by examining the arts of the early twentieth-century, for instance, it is possible to detect certain changes in progress. It is not as though the arts effect these changes *per se*, but through their essentially radical nature, they exhibit more readily the symptoms of cultural change and the tensions inherent between the desire to keep things as they are—to resist change and to protect social order as we know it—and the compulsion to redress those aspects of culture that repress, stifle, even merely pinch at parts of each of us, as members of our own culture.[11]

By seeing the visual arts of the avant-garde seep into the poetry of contemporary poets, in this case that of Marianne Moore, I would argue that we can thereby isolate cultural shifts. Certainly the poetry of Moore is critical of her culture, as I will argue in this book. However, she was deeply invested in this culture and often resorted to abstraction as a method to conceal her irritation with repressive or unfulfilling social and/or historical treatment of not just women but the underprivileged, the racially discriminated against, even just the unappreciated.

Any undertaking that examines the relationship between literature and the visual arts calls out for a rationalization for using this comparison at all. While the debate continues to come to no apparent resolution, it should seem by now that even if it is not possible to distinguish exact similarities between the overtly radically different media, it is fairly well established that the purpose of the various arts plays itself out in similar directions at certain times, such as in modernism.[12]

Like W. J. T. Mitchell, I am being so bold in this book as to conflate distinctions between the arts by adopting a formalist vocabulary.[13] Formalism as a critical tool has been justifiably suspect through its connections to New Criticism and to its rigid and inert approach to the arts. I think, however, that a formalism that accepts and even embraces cultural change could refresh a critical approach that continues to be useful, particularly in studies that take on interdisciplinary intersections.[14]

This variation on formalist criticism is, in fact, more flexible than other "traditional" interart critical methods, such as semiotics or symbolic structures, because it is not restricted to a one-to-one correspondence between a cultural artifact and its meaning, either linguistic or conceptual, a relationship that, once fixed by the scholar, is impervious to change.[15] As these cultural artifacts are an essential part of what constitutes meaning in culture, however, I am attempting to use formalism to be able to take advantage of what phenomena might seem easier to comprehend in one medium in order to explain occurrences or features that are less easy to grasp in another.

Formalist aesthetics can be developed in such a way as to admit social and historical change, as Ann Jefferson argues in "Literariness, Dominance and Violence in Formalist Aesthetics."[16] By explaining the failures and weaknesses in Roman Jakobson's formalist theory—but more, by deciphering his theoretical stance in such a way as to lay out the underlying similarities between his stance and Mikhail Bakhtin's—Jefferson brings formalist assumptions into a more pragmatic and socially interactive sphere because at root, both theorists require a belief in the transgressive nature of language, particularly artistic language.

Formalism can, I believe, be integrated into pragmatic discourse, as Nancy Fraser calls it, and it is this theory of discourse that drives current Moore scholarship.[17] For, as Bakhtin suggests, "the living utterance, having taken meaning and shape at a particular historical moment in a socially specific environment, cannot fail to brush up against thousands of living dialogic threads, woven by socio-ideological consciousness, around the given object of an utterance; it cannot fail to become an active participant in social dialogue."[18] While Bakhtin and Julia Kristeva both contend by extension that artistic language is transgressive of this "socially specific environment," and while other critics of Marianne Moore's poetry, such as Leigh Gilmore, embrace this attitude, I think that it is important to reinforce the sense here that Moore's poetry is not merely transgressive but that it engages directly with its environment and displays at once acceptance and adherence to this cultural situation, and disapproval as well as dismissal of it.[19]

For the purposes of this book, therefore, I am using the visual arts as an analogy for Moore's poetry in order to uncover the extent of her ambivalence about her own culture. It is not important to the relevance of this relationship whether Moore saw the artwork outlined here (although she saw much of it at least in reproduction) or whether she met these artists. Nor is it a question of these movements and techniques being "in the air" and so assimilated by Moore as a participant in her culture. The relationship between Moore's work and the visual arts is for me a route to gain access to her poetry from a new perspective. Therefore, there will be little attention in this book to Moore's biography. Much thorough and detailed work has been done on her involvement with the visual arts; no serious work can be done on it at this point without careful attention to Linda Leavell's thoroughly researched and argued book on Moore's place as an American artist both artistically and biographically.[20]

In this book I argue that it was through techniques of abstraction that Moore found the freedom to be critical of oppressive aspects of her own culture, criticism that she felt unable to express overtly (and that, therefore, does not appear in her letters, diaries, or other archival materials).[21] By dismantling narrative through methods of cubism, with its attention to crushed perspective, through the practice of collage which appears in Moore's poetry in the form of reshaped quotations, through the dada invention of photomontage, which incorporates spliced images into one composition, and through the surrealist attempt to comprehend the past through artifacts of the present, Moore systematically undermined social conventions and attitudes that she found stifling or, for her, even worse, unimaginative.[22] It is for this purpose that I base this examination of Moore's work on her early poetry.[23] I am looking for symptoms in her style that find reflection in the visual arts that were coming to fruition concurrently, in order to decipher the underlying critical intent of her poetry.

Cultural Critique and Abstraction

1
The Veil of Abstraction: Cultural Critique and the Imagination

Marcel Duchamp had four paintings in the New York Armory Show of 1913: *Le Roi et la reine traversées par des nus en vitesse*, *Portrait de joueurs d'échecs*, *Jeune Homme triste dans un train* and *Nu descendant un escalier*, all of which he had executed between 1911 and 1912. The striking scandal/success of Duchamp's work in this show brought it to the attention of a wide segment of American society. Duchamp enhanced this notoriety by moving to New York on a relatively permanent basis in 1915, by engaging in such stunts as portraying the transvestite character RRose Sélavy, and by creating his series of readymades. In an important and surprising way, Duchamp's work finds its parallel in Marianne Moore's poetry. His painting represents the avant-garde rejection of the bourgeois establishment.[1] Moore's work, too, in its radicalization of form, but more importantly in its searing cultural critique, endeavors to undermine oppressive social institutions and preconceptions. At the same time both artists would inspire a new culture through the underlying moral subjects of their work. In this paradox of radical form and moral content we see how social institutions change and the crucial role that the verbal and visual arts play in that change.

The Duchamp painting that provoked the most scandalous reception at the Armory show in New York, Boston, and Chicago, garnering such descriptions as "splinter salad," was *Nude Descending a Staircase, No. 2*.[2] This painting depicts the stages of the movement of a human figure down some stairs, as its title suggests. This figure has to change its stance radically as it descends, and Duchamp represents these shifts in

Marcel Duchamp (1887–1968). *Nude Descending a Staircase, No. 2*, 1912. Oil on canvas, 58 X 35 in. Philadelphia Museum of Art, Louise and Walter Arensberg Collection (Photo: Philadelphia Museum of Art).

balance and movement as the figure lifts successive feet in its downward progress. Its head is tilted downward, not in depression but in order to see where it is going. The artist rendered this figure as if it were drawn, rather than painted, so that the shape of the figure resembles small cut pieces of balsa wood rather than the smoother curves of the actual human shape.

The composition of the painting incorporates the diagonal of the stairs, with the figure more bunched toward the top step and lengthening out toward the bottom until it stretches from the bottom of the canvas almost to the top along the right side. Because the figure is slightly stooped at the top, however, the grouping of these varied depictions of its movement produces a pyramid effect, as its head stays near the center of the canvas while its feet swing out and extend from side to side.

In this painting Duchamp purports to adhere to traditional notions of painting by presenting the classical academic nude, an image that is generally a depiction of a female in a sexually available pose. It is possible that one level of the painting is just that, a representation of a naked woman, perhaps of Venus or of an angel, two of the few nudes who appear in motion. But on other levels of analysis, this painting thwarts conventions, and thereby the bourgeoisie, through the palette sapped of vibrancy and by allowing mere suggestion to carry the weight of the content matter of the painting.

The form of the painting, however, is only a part of its ultimate rejection of society. By its very representation of a woman in movement, and in particular a woman on a staircase, Duchamp's *Nude* defies bourgeois standards for female behavior. As I just mentioned, the standard form for the female nude in painting is as a sexually available object.[3] Duchamp flouts this convention by presenting a woman in motion—she is not merely an object of desire over which men can have ultimate power by removing her agency; instead she controls the narration, as it were, of the painting. Not only that, Duchamp presents this woman at a moment at which she normally has power over her audience: her entrance into society. She is still on display, but she has control over that display simply because she is in motion.[4] She is impossible to objectify when she is not presented as a mere static figure, one that is sexually available.

An even more compelling method behind Duchamp's subversion of bourgeois culture is his omission from this nude image of any overtly sexual characteristics. The complete shattering of this figure precludes the detail necessary in the depiction of sexual attributes.[5] This nude could, in fact, be a representation of a male figure. By doing this, by removing any hint of sexuality from this painting, Duchamp denies society its ability to objectify women.

Because Marianne Moore's work is so modest and because she is so successful at camouflaging her real purpose in her poems, little critical attention has been paid until recently to her equally radical nature, but the dramatic increase in attention to her work is in the process of changing this mistaken impression of her.[6] Cynthia Hogue, Cristanne Miller, and Sandra Gilbert, in particular, have examined Moore's public presentation and its undermining effect on a view of her poetry as avant-garde. Hogue discusses at length Moore's effort to "disown" "authorial presence" through Moore's own description of her publishing process that masks her truly professional, ambitious, and radical poetry through her adoption of a personal tone dismissive of its own potentials.[7] Miller critiques the view of Moore as self-effacing by suggesting that "Moore's non-'authorial,' abstract, shifting representation of identity or self [is] necessarily conjoined with, not effacing, a distinctive, idiosyncratic, and personal presence."[8] It is this radicality, as exhibited both through the formal qualities of her work and through its socially critical nature, however, I would contend, that aligns Moore's poetry with the work of the dadaists and the cubists, and which lends her work coherence by seeing it through the techniques of collage and photomontage.

I am going to argue in this book that Moore's poetry, unlike that of many of her compatriots (Wallace Stevens, for instance), is primarily avant-garde in nature as opposed to modernist.[9] I refer here to the split between modernism and the avant-garde, a split originating with the aestheticism movement, which entailed a rupture of art from its engendering culture. Art became increasingly isolated from bourgeois society in its rejection of bourgeois convention, but the result was to increase its powerlessness within that society.[10] As a result, modernist art became so involved in the form of its work that the form became the work's content.[11] The result of this situation was to remove the possibility for cultural or social change, at least that instigated through the arts, because art's topic became itself rather than the social or political.

Many theorists, particularly Theodor Adorno, have proposed that a major earmark of modernist art was the emphasis of form over the content, that as artists became increasingly interested in formal innovation, they finally transformed the form of the work into its content.[12] This is perhaps the case with painters such as the abstract expressionists whose paintings were able to focus entirely on the quality and texture of the paint itself. But I believe that for most artists, and certainly for Marianne Moore, form never overtakes the content of the work; it is exceptionally difficult for a work of art to remove iconicity entirely.[13]

Iconicity in the visual arts is, traditionally speaking, the extent to which an image represents or is similar to something in reality. It normally refers to the mimetic characteristic of an image. In interart

Kasimir Malevich (1878–1935). *Suprematist Composition: White on White*, c. 1918. Oil on canvas, $31\frac{1}{4}$ X $31\frac{1}{4}$ in. The Museum of Modern Art, New York (Photo: The Museum of Modern Art).

discussions, however, and in particular, in discussions relating to the emergence of abstraction in modernism, the meaning of iconicity shifts in order to encompass symbolic rather than literal referentiality so that the abstract work retains iconographic intention; it is merely that the intention has reconfigured itself so that what the icon symbolizes is less the external world than ideas with a relatively more internal focus.[14]

A telling example of the unlikelihood that a work of art, visual or verbal, could lose its iconic function is Charles Altieri's comparison of one of Kasimir Malevich's paintings to Moore's poetry.[15] This depiction of a square does not pretend to be a classically mimetic landscape, one that would be acceptable to the bourgeoisie, but it remains iconic in that it depicts *something*, in this case a square. In the same way, while she will manipulate form for a variety of purposes, Moore will never allow form to take over the position of the work's content. While this continued contact with traditions of content forces Moore to adhere to both the liberating and confining aspects of the conventions of her culture, it yet enables her to critique that culture, to redress its failings, from within, as it were. Heuving identifies this project of Moore's by saying that "Moore can engage the meanings of the larger literary tradition and system of representation," and, I believe, the culture as a whole, "without having to assume a singular or identificatory (specular) stance." Part of Moore's ability to do so, Heuving argues, and I concur, is her effort to "encounter and engage in symbolic discourse while maintaining a position 'elsewhere,'" as in "Poetry," where she places herself in the position of the audience rather than of the poet, as I argue further on in this chapter.[16]

This theory both supports and rejects Adorno's formal aesthetic theory. Because he reifies form, Adorno must allow it primacy in modernism, and because he believes that art's role in society is to subvert the "petrified and alienated reality" of the bourgeoisie, he must allow form to be the active force behind this subversion.[17] This overemphasis on form, however, could only work if it were possible to have an art that could be purely noniconic. The avant-garde, however, refused to divorce itself from bourgeois culture because a complete separation would prevent art from responding to, arguing against, or creating change in that culture. Instead, the avant-garde remained socially invested.[18] It reintegrated art into culture while it critiqued the culture at the same time. The avant-garde needed to remain in close contact with the bourgeoisie in order to break it down and attempt to reinvent it in a less stifling form.[19]

What the art of the avant-garde became, then, was an avenue toward establishing and identifying cultural meaning, a meaning that could change and adapt itself to the needs of the artists, or especially of those whose needs were not being met by the status quo. In addressing this artistic motive, I would like to revise Clifford Geertz's contention that culture is "an assemblage of texts" by positing that poetry and other art forms are assemblages of culture, that they are composed of cultural artifacts from widely disparate sources, and that, by examining art, we can determine to a certain extent the composition of a culture.[20] Again, just as Geertz says that "cultural forms can be treated as texts, as imaginative works built out of social materials," I would hold that imaginative works, that is, works of art, both literary and visual, are also "built out of social materials" and, as such, are products of the culture that allowed, and even enabled, their composition.[21]

Moore, in fact, uses Geertz's main method of symbolic anthropology: "thick description." Geertz defines thick description as description of the "stratified hierarchy of meaningful structures in terms of which [actions] are produced, perceived, and interpreted and without which they would not . . . exist."[22] The classic example of Geertz's technique is his essay on Balinese cockfights in *The Interpretation of Cultures*. He believes that by describing in extensive detail a particular cultural ritual, he can theorize about the symbolic structure of the entire culture. Moore's adaptation of "thick description" reveals itself in her poetry in the form of close attention to detail, to the white and black patterns on the lizard's tail in "Plumet Basilisk," to the ant's meanderings in "Critics and Connoisseurs," and to the "toilet-boxes" in "The Jerboa" with "the pivoting / lid incised with a duck-wing // or reverted duck head" (CP 11).

These details brought into Moore's poetry are not simply an effort to create the visual through the verbal but are, in fact, a part of her attempt not only to depict and create her culture but to define it. For, as the psychologist Jerome Bruner says, "culture and the quest for meaning within culture are the proper causes of human action," and this motivation is particularly true for artists.[23] In considering social change, though, the artist must become particularly aware of the power that culture has over language through its access to and even origination of meaning, and how meaning develops over time and becomes seemingly inexorable.[24]

In this context, too, recent Moore criticism places her poetry more immediately in the fray of tension between cultural change and relatively more constant institutions. Hogue identifies Moore's "effort to change the dominant social order."[25] Carolyn A. Durham argues that Moore has an "investment in social and political reality."[26] Rachel Blau DuPlessis contends that "social materials and cultural narratives saturate poetic texts," including those texts of Marianne Moore's.[27] Miller cites Foucault's treatise on power relations: "Where there is power, there is resistance, and yet, or rather consequently, this resistance is never in a position of exteriority in relation to power."[28] The most important aspect of this change in critical attitude toward Moore's work is its contention that Moore is intentionally and forcefully producing a poetry that promotes and actively engages social change.

In developing new meanings within culture, the avant-gardists freed language from the power that meaning had over them in order to create new meaning structures.[29] This action enabled the artists to take on power within the prevailing culture, a culture that had hitherto denied them entry to it.[30] The first effect of this revisionary freedom of language and of the image, however, was that of abstraction, the type of abstraction developed through such techniques as collage and photomontage, an abstraction that rejected the sequential character of narrative on which the bourgeois culture relies.

Abstraction was attractive to the avant-gardists for several reasons, the first of which was probably just to annoy and provoke the bourgeoisie. Beyond that, however, was the feeling that representation had been co-opted too thoroughly by the bourgeoisie and needed to become much more multivalent in order to recompose the conventions of the prevailing culture.[31] Important here, too, is the continual power of the bourgeoisie, a threat that was often too apparent to the artists. Abstraction provided them with the opportunity of cultural critique with the advantage of less fear of reprisal in the form of social condemnation as abstraction masks the subversive intent of the artist.

This discussion may not seem overtly related to an analysis of Marianne Moore's poetry, the poetry of a woman who never married, who lived continuously in America, primarily in Brooklyn (with her mother until that woman died), the model, in short, of the bourgeois dame herself. However, Moore was always aware of current developments in the arts. As my chapter on collage will show, she kept a scrapbook of the notorious Armory Show of 1913; she wrote art reviews for *The Dial* magazine, both before and when she was its editor; she went to museums often; she socialized with artists such as the Zorachs and with other artworld figures such as Monroe Wheeler, the curator at the Museum of Modern Art, and she occasionally met with members of the Others group.[32] As with the New York dadaists, Moore was a part of the changing American artistic scene, one that admitted abstraction as a method of social change.[33]

Marianne Moore's poetry defies cultural institutions in much the same way as Duchamp's painting and sculpture do. Not only is her poetic form radical enough to disturb the conventions of its audience, but her content is sharply critical of those conventions as well. Even so, perhaps because she was a woman and so more vulnerable to social constraints, Moore felt compelled to conceal her radical intentions behind various veils, one of which is abstraction.[34] Poetic abstraction allowed her to produce enough disjuncture in her narrative that the overt message of social critique becomes blurred, protecting her from facing the horror that her subversive message would induce in her more conventional audience.[35]

Often this elusiveness on Moore's part appears in her poetry through indeterminant meanings, some of which call into question the poem's existence from the very beginning. The first sentence of "To a Snail," for instance, undermines the poem from the start in two ways (O 23). Firstly, by starting the line with "If," Moore establishes the possibility that "'compression is the first grace of style'" does not exist, and even that compression might *not* be the first grace of style, in which case she forces us to question what the "first grace of style" might be. Secondly, Moore retreats from her own, already tentative position by immediately drawing a quotation from another source into the poem, as if to say that she does not herself believe in this statement, or at least is unwilling to accept responsibility for it. These overlapping measures of retreat on the part of the poet illustrate her constant denial of her also ever-present rebellion against the pressures of bourgeois culture.

Moore explains what she means by compression in the next sentence of the poem: "Contractility is a virtue / as modesty is a virtue." She compares here the physical action of drawing into oneself with the psychological characteristic of unpretentiousness.[36] Since Moore's topic in this poem is also style, it makes sense to relate her approval of the snail's ability to contract to her goal in poetic composition: that a good poem is "compressed."

It is this compression that, to a large degree, gives Moore's poetry a place, both technically and philosophically, in the avant-garde of the early twentieth century. Compression excises the connectives in her poetry so that she can disrupt logical narrative and embrace the abstraction of the cubists and dadaists and reconfigure the techniques of collage and photomontage into the verbal medium of poetry. Yet, as an apparently conventional and conforming American, Moore must strive as hard as the dadaists in Weimar Germany to cover her subversive tracks, for the censorship of the bourgeoisie is, while stifling, even more brutal than that of the politically corrupt.

Moore continues this poem with a statement that reinforces the notion that she feels compelled to conceal her true meaning in poetry:

> It is not the acquisition of any one thing
> that is able to adorn,
> or the incidental quality that occurs
> as a concomitant of something well said,
> that we value in style,
> but the principle that is hid.
>
> (O 23)

What is most important to Moore in her poetry is not the embellishments of the poetic form, nor even the pleasure of beautifully rendered phrases, but "the principle that is hid," the secreted ethical standards of the poem and of the poet herself.[37] The overall style of poetry, therefore, is not as important to Moore as is her belief that a poem must have a message to convey and that that message must be concealed. The words "value" and "principle" merit discussion here because they address important issues in Moore's working career. Moore's notion of ethics is often related to the standard Judeo-Christian dictums for behavior because of her conventional Protestant upbringing and brother's career as a clergyman. Instead, I would argue, she developed her own sense of ethics more closely related to those that Kristeva describes in *Revolution in Poetic Language*. Kristeva identifies ethics in art as occurring when the artist is able to focus less on his or her self or on his or her topic in favor of the actual process of the artwork and of the artwork's context. Kristeva explains this as follows:

> "Ethics" should be understood here to mean the negativizing of narcissism within a *practice*; in other words, a practice is ethical when it dissolves those narcissistic fixations (ones that are narrowly confined to the subject) to which the signifying process succumbs in its socio-symbolic realization. Practice, such as we have defined it, positing and dissolving meaning and the unity of the subject, therefore encompasses the ethical. The text, in its signifying disposition and its signification, is a practice assuming all positivity in order to negativize it and thereby make visible the process underlying it.[38]

In "To a Snail," as well as in the rest of her poetry, Moore creates a technique of poetry that leaves its process exposed: the style—her lack of connectives, her use of quotations, her abrupt enjambments—becomes the concealment for her understated purpose, her quiet policy that art's function is to reconsider the meaning created within the cultural context. This attitude places her in the avant-garde agenda that is always forcefully moral, as the extensive production of manifestos by the avant-garde artists dictating proper behavior indicates.

The last three lines of "To a Snail" represent Moore at her most elusive, a quality enhanced here by two uncited quotations. "The principle that is hid" is "in the absence of feet, 'a method of conclusions.'" Essentially the poet is referring to a fundamental issue in writing poetry: how to end a poem. Her amusement is apparent in telling the snail that having no feet at all is one way to end itself; having no conclusion is one way to end a poem.[39] "'A knowledge of principles,' / in the curious phenomenon of your occipital horn" shows that the purpose of a poem is as odd as the constantly reacting projections out of the snail's head. Careful analysis makes the poem's purpose apparent, but it can just as easily submerge itself into the poem's surface, just as the snail's "horns" alternate protrusion with complete submersion into the surface of the snail's head.

Moore's unembellished style in this poem, coupled with her primly moral tone, glosses over the true message that she is presenting. The purpose of the poem is socially directed for her, but as she is hesitant to be overt in her criticism of culture, she must prevail on poetic style to veil her intentions. Form might be expedient, as she contends in "The Past is the Present," but it is increasingly essential to a poet who uses the abstraction that formal innovations engender to conceal her disapproval of various confining features of a strongly bourgeois culture.

"To a Snail" presents another issue in modernist aesthetic theory, that of the form/content controversy. Moore's work, while vigorously involved in abstraction and innovative formal issues, can never abandon overt content sufficiently to foreground form exclusively.[40] What the continued reliance on content does for Moore, and for many other modernists, is to allow her to use form to diffuse her attack on social conventions by masking her critique, a mask that is necessary given the powerful influence of the status quo in American culture. In fact, through her adherence to scientific methods of classification, Moore creates an ostensible alliance between herself and the bourgeois reliance on rationality and objectivity, one that she must always undermine through her abstraction, which serves to fracture narrative and to critique the bourgeoisie through her richly moral aphorisms.[41]

"The Plumet Basilisk" is an example of how Moore manages to make her professed scientific method an actual tool of subversion (CP 20–24). On the surface, this poem is a catalog of lizards from different parts of the world; it presents their appearance as well as their behavior. The problem is that Moore cannot restrict herself to mere description. The Costa Rican lizard "can be 'long or short, and also coarse or fine at pleasure.'" The quotation is from an article on Chinese dragon myths, but neither the original phrase, nor Moore's inclusion of it, makes logical sense in terms of the appearance or behavior of either a dragon or a lizard.

The Malay lizard section incorporates the lyrical into the scientific, thereby shifting the ground from the objective into the imaginative: "Floating on spread ribs, / the boat-like body settles on the / clamshell-tinted spray sprung from the nut meg tree—minute legs / trailing half akimbo." The repeated *b*'s from "ribs," "boat-like" and "body," and the *sp*'s from "spray" and "sprung" jar against the arrhymthic "clamshell-tinted," while the rigid syllabics of the poem set up odd enjambments such as "the unnutritious nut- // tree." The lyrical style of poetry has a long tradition, and so Moore's use of it in this poem does nothing to critique her society. However, by setting up the poem with the tone of the objective cataloguer, and by then disrupting this cool rational description with the transcendental leap of the imagination, Moore disrupts the sequential form of the narrative, removing the poem from its adherence to codes of convention.

Moore uses unlikely tangents to effect the same rupture in the narrative later in the poem. In order to explain the "tuatera" lizard, Moore veers oddly to Denmark to describe the steeple over the bourse in Copenhagen that "is roofed by two pairs of dragons standing on / their heads—twirled by the architect—so that the four / green tails conspiring upright, symbolize four-fold security." There are indeed four upside-down dragons whose tails spiral upward to create the steeple of the bourse in Copenhagen, but their place in this poem is a mystery. A poem that purports to be rational, to adhere to bourgeois notions of conformity, should not deviate this far from its course. This tangent is a subversion, then, a dismissal of objectivity; the poem takes objectivity as one of its subjects and redirects it. It is in this way that Moore takes on her own culture—she uses its tools directly in order to denigrate it.

The last section of the poem confirms the poet's subversive stance. The first stanza begins properly, as if in a story (having just returned from a tangent): "now. . . as / I have said." The tone is matter-of-fact; its message is perfectly normal, even prosaic. The problem is that from this moment until the penultimate stanza, the poem slips into the ecstasy of the transcendental, entirely rejecting the bourgeois belief in the rational.[42] Much of this transcendental nature is induced through Moore's attempt to enter the visual and aural through the medium of language. The musical becomes essential here, with a

> galloped
> ground-bass of the military drum, the squeak of bag-pipes
> and of bats. Hollow whistled monkey-notes disrupt
> the castanets. Taps from the back of the bow sound odd on
> last year's gourd,
>
> or when they touch the
> kettledrums. . .

(CP 22)

and later:

> spider-clawed fingers can twang the
> bass strings of the harp, and with steps
> as articulate, make their way
> back to retirement on strings that
> vibrate till the claws are spread flat.

(CP 23)

Even more important in this context, however, is that this vibrantly alive lizard is intensely shy and fearful; it looks fierce but needs to hide:

> Thinking himself hid among the yet unfound jade ax-heads,
> silver jaguars and bats, and amethysts and
> polished iron, gold in a ten-ton chain, and pearls the size of pigeon-eggs,
>
> he is alive there
> in his basilisk cocoon beneath
> the one of living green; his quicksilver ferocity
> quenched in the rustle of his fall into the sheath
> which is the shattering sudden splash that marks his temporary loss.
> (CP 24)

This quick submersion into safety is the equivalent of Moore's escape into the obtuseness of abstraction. She has equal "quicksilver ferocity," as shown by her unhesitant aspirations for the transcendental away from the objectively rational, but must hide it for fear of reprisal from her own culture. The "loss" is the cost of removing herself from adherence to the status quo, but it is only "temporary" and will not put her at risk. The poem's conclusion with an image of repression of the vitally engaged lizard represents the repression of the equally vitally engaged poet, who must "dive," throw herself into social and political disapproval but concealing herself in the very act of doing so, as the jerboa must freeze when in open exposure, as I will discuss later.

Moore reinforces this impression of conflict through the push-pull tension of the basilisk's behavior, in what Heuving refers to as "moments of appearance and disappearance."[43] The "appearance" reflects the poet's urge to assert herself and her denial of repression; the "disappearance" depicts the fear that the primary urge induces, a fear of reprisal for overt criticism of convention. Robin Gail Schulze sees this poem, along with "The Jerboa" and "The Frigate Pelican," as an expression of "the desire to strip the world free of conventional fictive coverings."[44] I argue instead that Moore relies on "fictive coverings" to protect herself from punishment arising from a flouting of cultural tradition, a form of protection that she sometimes carried so far as to exclude (hide) poems from collections of her poetry, as with "Roses Only."

Moore refrained from including "Roses Only" in her *Complete Poems*, but it is a poem that illustrates her social investment. This poem, written in 1917, appeared in the 1924 *Observations* and again in her 1935 *Selected Poems*, but it was not included in later collections. It is of course possible that Moore let this poem go because she did not feel it was up to her poetic standards. I believe, however, that this poem came too close to an overt criticism of cultural conventions, particularly those determining standards of female appearance and behavior, for Moore to feel comfortable including it. One of the reasons for this discomfort may have been because this poem, as a very early one, draws in no quotations from other sources, so that it has no method of deflecting responsibility for its purpose away from the author, as do many of her other poems.

Whatever the reason for Moore's exclusion of this poem from later collections, it has not prevented intensive scholarly debate about it in the last few years. DuPlessis, Hogue, and Heuving are just a few of the critics to address "Roses Only" in conflicting manners.[45] They all acknowledge the parodical roots of the poem as a courtly love poem, but while Heuving argues that the poem "addresses the problem of women's representation as other by establishing the subjectivity, assertiveness and intelligence of such a traditionally feminine other as the rose,"[46] Hogue contends that "the text enacts how the repression of difference is constituent of identity."[47] One is trying to suggest that the poem lays out sexual identity and difference more sharply, while the other wants to say that identity formation is itself reliant on diminishing this difference. I would suggest that Moore is in a sense operating from both of these directions at once. By identifying cultural stereotypes of female beauty and by calling them into question, she is emphasizing how differently women are treated culturally, but by stressing female spiritual and intellectual beauty in this poem, Moore transcends gender difference and stereotype in order to revalue women.

This poem is more avant-garde than modernist in its relationship to social issues. A contrast with imagism serves to explain this distinction. Imagism tried to present an object in its static form, as a still life. We see this in William Carlos William's wheelbarrow, Wallace Stevens's blackbirds, H. D.'s rose.[48] Moore repeatedly described objects with a certain degree of objectivity, like the imagists, but unlike them she could never resist applying a moral or critical tone of some sort onto the object; it always had to represent something more than just the image of itself for her.[49]

H. D.'s "Sea Rose" is a perfect imagist poem. The work rests entirely on the rose and how it looks in its seaside setting: "Stunted, with small leaf, / you are flung on the sand /. . . that drives in the wind." The only authorial comment in the poem is the wonder that the dried and sandy flower could still bear a perfume: "Can the spice-rose / drip such acrid fragrance / hardened in a leaf?" Because the poem is so centered on the single object, the focused still life of the rose, it retains the essential qualities of the imagist poem.[50]

Moore's "Roses Only," however, is not only a description of the rose; it also discusses beauty's role in society and the contradiction in the rose between its beautiful flower and its prickly thorns, placing it overtly in a cultural context and increasing the complexity of the poem through the development of allegorical levels.

Moore begins the poem by saying that "beauty is a liability" and then says "in view of the fact that spirit creates form we / are justified in supposing / that you must have brains" (O 41). The second-person address of the poem refers primarily to the rose itself, but underlying this direct subject is a reference to women and the relationship between their appearance and their intelligence.[51] Moore is subverting here the normal American supposition that beauty indicates stupidity in women, which makes it a "liability." We in our culture do not take beautiful women seriously—they are adornments only, incapable of conceptual activity. Moore's conversion of this cultural bias unveils its inherent flaws by supposing the reverse: why wouldn't a person of exceptional physical beauty be therefore one of spiritual beauty, and so one of intellectual prowess?

Moore's furious criticism of this cultural prejudice surfaces in her next sentence, in which she calls the rose "stiff and sharp," turning the woman into a phallus and thereby attempting to give her social power.[52] Her anger at the rose's [woman's] position is also apparent when she describes it as "conscious of surpassing by dint of native superiority and liking for everything / self-dependent, anything an / ambitious civilization might produce" (O 41). The rose [woman] is aware of the fact that her natural talents and independence make her more wonderful than anything that human beings could fabricate. The stress on "self-dependence" is especially telling here; a woman who needs no one other than herself to be what she is, who does not require a husband to provide her with an identity, is "superior." This message contradicts that presented by bourgeois culture, a society that contends that a woman is nothing without her man, that it is his accomplishments, career, and social status that shape her own, and that a woman who is self-reliant is better than one who is dependant.

This rose, however, is too "reserved" to rectify the misconceptions that people have about her, which they take from mere "observations" of her, and it is "idle" for her to "attempt" to change these spot impressions. It is impossible for the rose [woman] to be overt in asserting herself in her own culture, to notify society that she merits more respect, that she deserves attention as a "delightful happen-so."[53] This entrapment in passivity recalls the attitude of self-effacement that Moore effects in her own public persona, as I have indicated earlier with reference to Miller's and Hogue's work.

While the rose cannot be overtly assertive, she does have the ultimate weapon of thorns to protect her place in her culture. It is not because the rose is beautiful that Moore finds her "brilliant," it is because of her thorns, without which the flower would be a "mere peculiarity." The thorns of the rose do not protect it from natural predators, such as worms, storms, or mildew, but from the "predatory hand," the human being. The rose as beautiful woman would here represent the ability of the woman to ward off easy dismissal, and more especially, easy co-option by the prevailing culture. Instead, the thorns of the rose guard "the / infinitesimal pieces of your mind," preventing this culture from exerting complete dominance over the inner subversion of the woman. In doing so, Moore creates a poetry that, as Heuving puts it, "confronts the problematic of constructing a universal consciousness dispossessed of as well as refusing traditional representational conventions that would enable her to do so."[54] The woman whom she depicts in this poem no longer needs to rely on behavior or appearances dictated by the status quo.

The thorns of the rose, then, represent the cultural critique upon which Moore has embarked. They are the "best part" of the rose because they keep the "audience" at bay: "it is better to be forgotten than to be remembered too violently." It is better not to pick the rose than to be pricked by it. As with "The Plumet Basilisk," Moore ends this poem with the instruction that women would do better to hide quietly and to mask their denigration of the oppressive aspects of culture in order to undercut that culture more effectively. Cultural approbation is, after all, a cruel force to face. It is possible to get away with mild pricking of that culture, however, if that critique is concealed by physical beauty or by the veil of abstraction.

This poem resists the static quality of the imagist poem by its insistence on political activism.[55] Unlike H. D.'s view of the sea rose as just that—a rose—Moore's rose represents the stereotypical position of women in bourgeois culture, a position in which women are assessed according to their physical merits. Few would take the time to look more closely at women, as "Roses Only" states, to "confute presumptions resulting from observation," to assess women's abilities as they really are rather than as they are reputed to be.

Moore's primary escape from the cultural repression that "Roses Only" represents was through the imagination. Moore used the poetic imagination to represent the transformative power of the arts over social tradition. Her original version of "Poetry," the one relegated to the "notes" section of her *Complete Poems*, presents not only her view of the operations of the imagination but that of twentieth-century American poets in general (CP 266–67).[56] As with Moore's abstraction through particulars, her investment in the power of the imagination in the arts is convincing proof of her denial of bourgeois conventions—there is no room for the imagination in a society based on pragmatic, materialistic lifestyles.[57] Not only that, but the very fact that Moore reduced the overt presentation of this poem to a few lines in the body of this poetry collection illustrates her reluctance to admit her critique of the bourgeoisie and her reliance on the imagination to escape it.

By introducing this poem with "I, too, dislike it" (O 30), Moore acknowledges the inherent triviality of poetry; it fulfills no "practical" function and, therefore, has no apparent role in culture. Her ironic tone in this line, however, negates its surface meaning and reinforces her belief in the power of the imagination to find a place for poetry in establishing meaning in culture.

Even though there is much poetry that she does not like, Moore admits that there is "in / it after all, a place for the genuine." To Moore, "the genuine" is the most essential attribute of good art. She treats it the way Wallace Stevens treats his notion of reality—as poetry's goal. Unlike Stevens, though, Moore does not believe that poetry is transcendental;[58] its reason for existence is entrenched in its ability to capture a sincere response to life's experiences, those that accurately reflect the social context of the poet.

Moore believes that physical responses and instincts are "important . . . because they are / useful," not because they can be explained in the abstract terms of poetic analysis and criticism.[59] The "eyes / that can dilate, hair that can rise / if it must" are human reactions to external stimulae. Moore wants poetry to function in the same way—rather than being so complex and difficult that it connects only to our intellect, it should stimulate us also through our physical senses. When poetry becomes too abstract, "as to become un-/intelligible," it loses its audience because "we / do not admire what / we cannot understand" (O 30). The poem then lists animal behaviors that are as indecipherable as modern poetry: the upside-down bat, the rolling horse. Human behavior is equally difficult to comprehend: "the base- / ball fan, the statistician" (O 30). But these behaviors are admirable: even activities that lack a pragmatic purpose are "important" because they lend distinction to the variety found in nature and among human civilizations. Even the dullness of "'business documents and / / school-books'" are important to human existence, perhaps as a contrast to more exciting aspects of life. Despite our lack of comprehension of "phenomena," we must confront them repeatedly, following that human instinct to investigate and describe. Even though abstract poetry is obscure, Moore poses, it is worth our attention because it is no more difficult to understand than anything else around us: it remains a reflection of the changes in our culture.

One must make a distinction
however: when dragged into prominence by half poets,
the result is not poetry,
nor till the poets among us can be
"literalists of
the imagination"—above
insolence and triviality and can present

for inspection, "imaginary gardens with real toads in them,"
shall we have
it. In the meantime, if you demand on the one hand,
the raw material of poetry in
all its rawness and
that which is on the other hand
genuine, you are interested in poetry.

(O 30–31)

But, Moore says, there are dull things that really are useless, such as bad poetry, and it is bad poetry that makes her think at first that she "dislikes" the genre entirely. Poetry as a legitimate entity exists only when poets have learned to be "'literalists of the imagination'" and when they can create in their work "'imaginary gardens with real toads in them.'" These quotations, one from William Butler Yeats and the other unacknowledged but perhaps by Moore herself, are the key to Moore's poetics.

The Yeats quotation is from his discussion of Blake in *Ideas of Good and Evil*, in which he describes Blake as a "too literal realist of imagination, as others are of nature."[60] By this, Yeats is criticizing, yet admiring, Blake for wanting poetry and the visual arts to depict symbols in their naked state, without the embellishment of style or technique. For Moore, the essential goal of poetry is to explain the poem's purpose while excluding the "trivial" or the "insolent," those irrelevant or self-destructive elements of much of failed poetry.

The idea of the "'imaginary gardens with real toads in them'" explains the force of imagination necessary for poets to avoid uselessness. They must, in order to be able to write authentic poetry, create a world in their minds that appears to be real. The toads, then, are the fabrications of the artist and are so highly refined by the artist's imagination that they have become tangible; the toads are the result of the artist's attempt to render the abstract into the concrete, Moore's own poetic goal, a goal that also allows her to draw directly into her poems the subversion that the abstraction serves to shield.

This goal is, however, as Moore acknowledges, unattainable. The effort to reach it is poetry's only hope. As long as the poet maintains this effort honestly, poetry is at least "interesting." Poetry is "raw" because it cannot have the polish of reality seamlessly constructed out of the imagination; it is "genuine," though, because the good poet tries with integrity to attain this reality. This passage presents the double nature of the imagination: it can create a visual image—the garden—but it can also create new phenomena in the form of abstractions—the formally "real" toads. A "'literalist of the imagination'" is bent on using the imagination exactly as it evidences itself in the interior nature of the artist. The poet who can make use of this faculty without distortion will be true to the forces and transcendental qualities of the imagination.[61] The imagination, then, works to divorce the poet from stifling conventions, while the abstraction that the imagination induces masks that very social defection.[62]

The ending of this poem also reinforces the problem that Moore confronted in her work: the inescapable tension between codified social convention and the urge to modify that convention so that it is less irksome to the individual. Moore wants poetry to retain direct connections to her culture, to continue to be "genuine" (i.e., intelligible and reflective of her culture). But at the same time she cannot resist the gentle undercutting of that culture through the abstraction brought on by the imaginary.

The imaginary undermines bourgeois culture because it is no longer attached to the pragmatic; it is no longer materially useful. Yet, like the hair that rises for no practical purpose on the human nape, the imaginary seems to Moore to be one of those marvels of nature that should continue to exist merely to be understood. Even so, the imaginary, and its creation, the abstract, do have practical and political implications. As such, they are the earmarks of societal change, the disruption of bourgeois dogma that everything must have its use, and the movement away from the sheerly socially pragmatic toward the operations of the individual's interior. Moore's standard for pragmatism is itself abstract, in fact, and strives for the furtherance of life and the understanding of that life rather than the typical pragmatic stance that has interest only in the production of particular consequences.

Moore's poem "To Statecraft Embalmed" embodies her sense of frustration with this spiritual blindness of the bourgeoisie, encapsulated in this case in the bungled diplomatic negotiations that led to the First World War. But it also reveals her continual adherence to the ethics of the poet as I outlined above, that the poet's job is to transgress cultural imperatives in order to admit necessary cultural change. This poem is more overt in its message than many of Moore's, primarily because it addresses a more impersonal topic—current events—and embraces a more commonly accepted opinion of them than her poems usually do: that much of the war's occurrence was due to diplomatic incompetence.[63] This poem was the first of her poems to appear in *Others*, the literary magazine published by a group of avant-garde Americans that included Arensberg and Williams. Published in the first volume of the journal, in December 1915, the poem reflects Moore's disgust with the absurdity of the war.

The very title of the poem indicates Moore's sense of hopelessness in the war situation. If statesmanship is indeed "embalmed," it has died already, meaning that it no longer has any power over the current situation. In addition, diplomacy has been preserved as it is, so the possibility of its becoming more effective has been erased.

Moore's first line confirms her fury: "There is nothing to be said for you" (O 29). This dismissal of the entire diplomatic enterprise leaves us assured that Moore sees no hope for diplomacy's improvement. This line mimics that of "Poetry" as well: "I, too, dislike it." To begin a poem with such a final remark makes it halt abruptly before it can even start. This jarring commencement is, I believe, an indication of Moore's effort to disrupt normal social discourse, to cut through convention, so that she can work through methods of social change.

She keeps us going through the first line, however, by starting the next sentence at its end with "Guard." The word alone means that statecraft's first job is to protect. But to protect what? Individual countries? Human rights? These next two sentences, "Guard / Your secret. Conceal it under your hard / Plumage, necromancer," are the types of lines that led critics to argue that Moore's poetic intention was that of concealment and of her desire for protective armor, but reading closely makes clear that she is telling statecraft to do this, to hide its secret, and that it is statecraft that bears protective armor.

Moore's specific target in this poem appears to me to be the English or the French, for they each had Egypt as one of their colonies and would have used "'awnings of Egyptian / Yarn.'" Each country, too, faced extreme decline in power and fortune in the early twentieth century, what Moore refers to in this poem as a "once vivid sovereignty." Whichever country she depicts here, she decries its lack of vigor, its absence of firm purpose, its appearance of passivity in the face of inappropriate international behavior on the parts of other countries involved in the war.

Moore sees this statesman as an ibis, one of the sacred birds of Egypt. She selected this animal on several counts, I believe, one of which is its ungainly walking, what she describes as "stalking" and "half limping and half-ladyfied." As an Egyptian figure, the ibis represents the ancient Egyptian rituals of embalming that were so effective as to preserve bodies for millenia. Moore wants to emphasize in this poem the statesman as preserved and worshipped long after his vitality and effectuality have dissipated, with only a "death mask" to present to the world.

The ibis was the Egyptian god of learning and the inventor of writing, named Toth. It embodied the binaries of white and black, of life and death. Moore's selection of this animal for this poem reflects her sincere disgust with the powers of diplomacy. It had been a great profession; now, it was a mere shadow of the most valued use of great knowledge, the mediation for peaceful ends.

"O / Bird," Moore asks the diplomat, "shall Justice' faint, zigzag inscription— / Leaning like a dancer— / Show / The pulse of its once vivid sovereign?" (O 29). All that is left to proclaim the rights of people is a scarcely legible and toppling decree. This "faint" message is not just indistinct and dimly readable but weak and lustreless. The bird replies in the negative and wanders around, lifted from the grave, the "sarcophagus," talking endlessly but so ineffectually that it is as if the talk "wind[s] / Snow / Silence round us"; it goes nowhere and says nothing. The word "wind" here recalls the wrappings of a mummy yet reverberates with the element of wind whipping the chill snow through the scene. Moore can find nothing good about this statesman—how could he have the semblance of life yet be "so dumb," in the sense of silent as well as stupid?

Moore now selects aspects of the ibis's behavior that she finds most scandalous. "Discreet behavior" is not the way to act right now, even though it was once the standard of good taste, "the incarnation of dead grace." This diplomat, who cannot even see "the steep, too strict proportion / Of [his] throne," is not self-aware enough to understand how important his work is, how much it is affecting the rest of the world, how much power he has or how little use he is making of it. Because of this ineffectual behavior, the statesman will be forced to witness the failure of his efforts, in a Yeatsian apocryphal ending:

> you'll see the wrenched distortion
> Of suicidal dreams
> Go
> Staggering toward itself and with its bill
> Attack its own identity, until
> Foe seems friend and friend seems
> Foe.
>
> (O 29)

This is not a monster, "slouching towards Bethlehem," but a silly, preening bird that is so frivolous as to reduce itself to attack its own kind, inducing a kind of self-destruction in the process.

The tight syllabic and rhyming structure of this poem, the few odd enjambments, the lack of quotations, all produce a more overtly critical statement of principle than Moore normally allows herself. There is little abstraction here to use as a veil. I contend, though, that this poem further supports my argument that Moore used abstraction as a method to mask her cultural criticism, for when she directs the criticism toward subjects more personally influential, such as the work of writing or social institutions like marriage, she deflects attention away from the overt intentions of her poems, submerging these intentions by methods of abstraction, recreating them to disguise the underlying subversion.

This discussion leaves open the question of what cultural meaning is for Marianne Moore and of how avant-garde artists can attain social power through language or image in their work. I believe that Moore's poem "Novices" offers the answer to some of these questions, although not all of them.[64] Overall, the message of this poem is that dilettantes, people who are not entirely devoted to their work, do not understand the artist's role in subverting society in order to change it, and that the avant-gardist's job is not only to break down that society but to wrest power out of this rejection in order to offer solutions.[65] Often, we see this recreation in Moore's poetry through the avenue of her aphorisms. In this poem, however, she remains more overtly focused on how to train novices to do the real work of the artist (or, more likely, perhaps, to try to make novices stop interfering in the arts).

Moore first explains in this poem a major weakness in the novices' approach toward their art: "Novices / / anatomize their work / in the sense in which Will Honeycomb was jilted by a duchess" (O 71).[66] Will Honeycomb, Erickson explains, was a character fabricated by Addison and Steele for their *Spectator Club*.[67] Novices feel compelled, Moore believes, to take apart their work, to spend all their time thinking about the parts of the work instead of assessing the effects and purpose of the whole. This is similar, Moore believes, to the way in which Honeycomb must obsess about his failure with the duchess, an undeveloped relationship, rather than moving on to real relationships.

Moore determines that this inappropriate designation of relative importance is caused by "the little assumptions of the scared ego confusing the issue" (O 71). The novice does not have the sureness of quality or approach or purpose that the artist does. The novice cannot determine what issues are important in artmaking, and as the poem progresses, we will see that the appropriate issues are more socially and politically subversive than the novice would like.

Novices "do not know 'whether it is the buyer or the seller who gives the money'— / an abstruse idea plain to none but the artist, / the only seller who buys, and holds on to the money" (O 71). Moore is saying here that dilettantes are unaware of the compensatory nature of artmaking that the artist, in making art, replenishes him or herself and offers that product to the public. Even if the public "buys" the work (an actuality in the case of most of the visual arts), the artist retains it figuratively in the sense of what making that artwork has done for him or her.

The acerbic quality of Moore's tone only increases when she notes that "because one expresses oneself and entitles it wisdom, one is / not a fool. What an idea!" (O 71). Clearly, just referring to oneself as wise does not make that attribute viable. In fact, Moore contends, novices are deadly to art. They are "'Dracontine cockatrices'" with the power to kill art with their gaze. They are the dwellers of Plato's cave, with minds "'unlit by the half-lights of more conscious art'" (O 71).

These novices do not know how to determine the "right word," but more tellingly, they are "deaf to satire," a failing that Moore feels prevents them from exercising their brains but that also prevents them from having the ability to identify social problems, to depict and disparage these problems in their work, to pose solutions to those stifling aspects of their own cultures. This "deafness" also protects novices from "'that tinge of sadness about it which a reflective mind / always feels'" (O 71).

A major problem with dilettantes for Moore, however, is that they write for women but have no comprehension of women:

> they write the sort of thing that would in their judgment
> interest a lady;
> curious to know if we do not adore each letter of the alpha-
> bet that goes to make a word of it—
> . . . the counterpart to what we are:
> stupid man; men are strong and no one pays any attention;
> stupid woman; women have charm and how annoying they can be.
> (O 71)

This type of art diminishes women by addressing itself to "ladies," women who are frivolous and at leisure but who do not like to think, merely to look at the beauty of the work, thereby turning poetry into an image instead of reading and interpreting its message. Moore criticizes this incorrect preconception of women, as she does in "Roses Only," by remarking on the social inconsistency of male and female social roles. If a man is stupid but strong, few comment on his stupidity; if a woman is stupid but charming, everyone remarks on her stupidity.

Moore continues this poem by harpooning the idiocy of the dilettante: the most "wonderful" are "those / that write the most," who speak the most "languages"; they are the "supertadpoles of expression" (O 72). This last statement is an example of the satire or irony that Moore earlier says is missing from novices' poetry. The comparison of the novice with the hypercephaly of the tadpole, increased in size, actually shrinks the likelihood that the novice could use the fine skills of the artist in expression.

The rest of the poem represents almost exclusively what Moore proposes for the power of art in society and for the power of language in promoting freedom from the stifling confines of bourgeois convention. She uses the ocean as a metaphor for this occasion, much as she does recurrently in her poetry. Novices, she says, stay above the surf, by which she means that they avoid difficult material for their work. They will address Plato because that philosopher's writings are filled with "'much noble vagueness and indefinite jargon,'" so that they are not forced to be specific or to confront the philosopher's issues; they will write about the "recurring phosphorescence of antiquity," a surface phenomenon that requires a little history but very little depth (O 72).

What keeps these dilettantes out of deep water is their "suavity," their "willowy wit," characteristics that imply no substance. They will confront the "transparent equation of Isaiah, Jere- / miah, Ezekiel, Daniel," but, and this is most telling, they will not consider more difficult material. The reality is that these novices are "bored by 'the detailless perspective of the sea'. . . and its chaos of rocks" (O 72). The sea represents what is most difficult—the conceptual, the abstract, the transcendent—and these are the true subjects and avenues of poetry. The power of art enters here, where the novices leave it, and it is also at this juncture that the power of the imagination and its tool, language, finally confront the status quo with its reluctance to change.

The Hebrew language represents to Moore poetic language at its height. In its complexity, its fearlessness in engaging the most intricate, but also in its passionate beauty, this language conjoins with the sea at its most rough: crashing waves against the rocks. This moment in the poem is where the poet takes the most risk from possible overexposure and failure.[68] By trying to re-create the vibrant activity of the sea's breakers, Moore comes the closest to the cinematic of any of her poems. Clashing the metaphor of the sea and the Hebrew language as the model for the form of the poem, Moore envisions a glass thrown upon a wall with such force that light catches, as if in slow motion, the shattered fragments as they shear away in explosive reaction, "in which action perpetuates action, and angle is at variance / with angle" (O 72).[69]

In order to commit herself to this tour de force, Moore must remove herself from the sequential form of the narrative and from the highly confining forms of grammar. The last sentence, in fact, is a fragment, leaving the poem in the suspension of the "hiss" of foam on the beach as the wave has spent itself (this is certainly a climactic image). In doing so, Moore proves that language is as equally appropriate a tool for women as for men and that through the imagination, the power of language is effective in easing the confines of the bourgeoisie and in developing fulfilling and unrestrictive meaning within culture.

Language, the language of poets especially, has the ability to renegotiate power structures in a given culture—to subvert, as Heuving puts it "a specular/symbolic discourse."[70] Kristeva argues this point at great length in *Revolution in Poetic Language*. She writes:

> The text is able to explore the mechanism of rejection in its heterogeneity because it is a practice that pulverizes unity, making it a process that posits and displaces theses. . . . In every kind of society and situation, the text's function is therefore to lift the repression that weighs heavily on this moment of struggle, one that particularly threatens or dissolves the bond between subject and society, but simultaneously creates the conditions for its renewal.[71]

Kristeva theorizes that poetic language is transgressive of the social order, thereby providing access to a reassessment of that order and the possibility of its modification. Moore's argument in poems such as "Novices" is that poetic language in the hands of women is particularly effective in what Kristeva terms the "telescoping of the symbolic and the semiotic [to pluralize] signification or denotation" because gender difference automatically places female poets in opposition to the established order, making them more likely to see and critique discrepancies and injustices.[72]

In decrying in "Novices" those who take a superficial view of art and who rely on prejudice and lack of judgment when making it, Moore presents herself as a member of the avant-garde—those who, while ostensibly merely trying to annoy and shock the bourgeoisie, in fact found themselves in a sincere and totally committed group of artists who wanted to revitalize their engendering culture, to change it through the medium of the arts. Moore's work fits this agenda perfectly. Unlike many of these artists, however, she hesitated to critique society overtly and so relied on the shield of abstraction to deflect the social approbation that she called upon herself, the techniques for which I will be discussing in my next chapters on cubism, collage, and photomontage.

2

"Prismatic Color": Marianne Moore's Cubism

Modern poets responded to cubism directly, and poets from William Carlos Williams to Gertrude Stein developed poetic styles that show a direct influence on their work by this visual arts movement.[1] The cubist poets were trying to be as resistant to the dominating culture as the painters were, but where (as I will discuss further) the painters attempted to reject that culture through the addition of language to the canvas, the poets tried to effect the same rejection by performing the reverse action, by adding the visual arts to their language. Cubism was a distinctive movement for the poets because, unlike imagism, which leaves the eye and the artwork still, or vorticism, wherein the eye is still but the world moves, cubism presents the world as still and the eye as moving, a fact that allowed the poets to give their audience a more active role in the work itself. Alfred H. Barr Jr., reinforces this idea when he says that the cubists "might move around the object, but it remained static," forcing the viewer's eye to move also.[2]

Of the modern American poets, though, Marianne Moore is one of the most effective at transforming the ability of cubism to open up a multifaceted view to the single impression into the verbal form. She focuses closely on a subject, like the imagists, but she moves beyond the subject itself to encompass in the single frame of the poem the subject in its entirety—its physical characteristics, its historical import, its relation to its environment. Moore's poetry also proves the inherent flexibility of the verbal form of cubism; it is not constrained by mere physical appearance, as is the visual arts, but can open up the subject more fully to expose its interior operations and influences. By peeling open its subject in such a manner, however, cubism disrupts narrative qualities.

Poetry's role in modern art was critical because the poetic form can so easily drop narrative qualities.[3] Leo Steinberg explains the antinarrative quality of cubist art and, by extension, poetry in his stellar essay on Picasso's *Les Demoiselles d'Avignon*, "The Philosophical Brothel."[4] Steinberg contends that the lack of interaction between the figures in this painting destroys any narrative quality that it might have had. I would add to this that the refracted "light" of the prismatic effects of cubism, the crushed perspective that cubism embraces, and the repetition with variation involved in the production of cubism, whether verbal or visual, cause the subjects that the artists are representing to have no easily intelligible relation to each other, diminishing the possibility of consistent narration. This antinarrative quality of cubism is most apparent in Marianne Moore's poetry in her consistent compilation of unrelated images in unconnected juxtaposition.

Cubism is a special case in the modernist efforts at antinarrative because it introduced the written word into the visual arts as an abstract image or token. Graphics had appeared in paintings much earlier, as Michael Fried, in his work on Thomas Eakins and Stephen Crane, *Realism, Writing, Disfiguration*, has noted, but never with the overt goal of sheer abstraction. To Fried, "the proliferation of images of writing in Eakin's pictures may be seen both as representing an effort at containment—painting depicts writing and thereby masters it—and as an index of the less than complete success of that effort—writing investing painting and thereby escaping its control."[5] I would suggest that the cubists were investigating a similar idea, one that they took to a further extreme in the collage movement when they introduced actual type into the composition: the power of the bourgeoisie over cultural productions was embodied in the written word. By inserting graphics into their work, the painters were able to try to assert control over that part of culture that dominated them. At the same time, however, as Fried suggests, the artists were unable to exert full dominance over this culture; their co-option of the written word forced them to embrace that very culture that they were trying to resist.

While responding to its traditions, cubism criticizes them at the same time, partly through abstraction. As I discussed in chapter 1, Adorno feels that this criticism appears in art's rejection of the bourgeoisie. The late art historian Edward Fry reinforces this idea by saying that "cubism . . . displays the personal, socially alienated and antibourgeois characteristics of modern Western bourgeois high culture."[6] What these theories contend, therefore, is that cubism rejects the tenets of the bourgeoisie at the same time that it embraces them. As radical as this art form may have appeared at the time of its development, it yet embodied obvious relations to its engendering milieu.

The novelty that inspired cubism, and the poetry of the time, still relied on notions of representation through its continued adherence to traditional techniques of form and content, language and symbol. However, because of their investment in the idea that the foundation of aesthetic theory was representation, critics themselves have had to change their definitions of representation in order to make it continue to adhere to the new art forms. Nelson Goodman, for instance, insists that "resemblance disappears as a criterion of representation and structural similarity as a requirement upon notational or any other languages. The often stressed distinction between iconic and other signs becomes transient and trivial."[7] Goodman dismisses the standard belief that representation in the arts is or ever has been the effort toward capturing a mimesis of nature. Now representation is clearly no longer tied to what it represents; it has evolved into a new way of addressing the world. "Representing," Goodman says, "is a matter of classifying objects rather than of imitating them."[8] What Goodman is doing here, and what I believe poets such as Marianne Moore are doing, is rejecting nature or other standards for mimesis, but not rejecting representationality. Art continues to be representational, but on a more abstract basis, so that what it represents is not derived from the concrete world.

Kendall Walton concurs with Goodman in *Mimesis as Makebelieve* when he says that "to be representational is not necessarily to represent something. Not all representations have objects."[9] What critics such as Goodman and Walton have done then, in the service of cubism and the art movements that developed after it, is to denude representationality of its concrete subject matter. No longer does art have to be connected to nature in order to retain its all-important iconicity. Even so, the importance that critics continue to place on ideas of representation indicates their concern that art always be connected to a sense of the concrete, to its shadow or veil if nothing else. Moore's work exemplifies this effort perfectly because her poetry often feels as though it has a concrete basis, a strong connection to the detailed and mimetic image, but she subverts this apparent claim to traditions of representation by setting up her work more as a catalogue of images than as a focus on the images themselves.[10]

Fry, Altieri, and Steiner explain this dissolution of the root of representation as mimesis by severing representation from iconography.[11] Fry argues that the development of art photography freed painters from concerns with mimesis. By asserting that "in contrast to traditional painting cubism replaces the role of remembered iconographic texts with the memories of perceptual and cognitive experience . . . [t]hus the presence of an exactly requisite number of scrambled or displaced signs for, say, human features will generate a contextual reading of those signs and create the nonmimetic representation of a human face," Fry suggests that we take the pieces that cubism presents to us and reconfigure them into what is to us a recognizable form.[12]

Cubism continues to be representational, then, just not mimetic. Cubism never rejects art's major connection to its role as depictor of the culture from which it springs, but at the same time, it revises notions of representation that date back to Plato. As I suggested in the introduction, Altieri and Steiner theorize that iconicity has been transformed through the modernist movement so that it represents a "state" rather than a tangible scene—it has become more a spiritual depiction than a concrete one.[13]

This vigorous and continual modern reassessment of the roles of representation and iconography in cubism forced critics to address form because the content of cubism tended to be suppressed. Once representation is no longer determined by how well the artist depicts a scene using techniques of mimesis, how the artist depicts the scene becomes the critic's only method of discussing the artwork. John Goulding, in *Cubism: A History and an Analysis 1907–1914*, discusses the cubist artists' attitude toward form in their painting: "Feeling that traditional painting was exhausted, they took each of the elements that comprise the vocabulary of painting—form, space, colour and technique—and substituted for the traditional use of every one of them a new interpretation of their own."[14] An analysis of cubism for most critics becomes then an assessment of all formal features of painting—perspective, light, composition, continuity—and how these techniques conform to those of "traditional" work.

As I indicated earlier, Adorno's aesthetic theory suits the emphasis on form in modern poetry and painting. Through formal innovations, the cubists were able to create a new art form, one that relies on a disruption of narrative to propel it and that therefore undermines the bourgeois reliance on time-sequential narrative. The cubist painters Pablo Picasso and Georges Braque disturbed the "narrative" of the painting in the same way that Marianne Moore uprooted the narrative of the poem: by condensing perspective, by repeating and overlapping lines to indicate images, and by refracting "light."

Alfred Stieglitz loaned a Picasso drawing to the organizers of the Armory Show, an exhibit of avant-garde work of which Moore was well aware, as the next chapter demonstrates.[15] This drawing came out of Picasso's analytical stage of cubism, so-called because of its distortion of rounded forms into geometrical shapes, its emphasis on straight lines over curves, and its reliance on systematic shading as opposed to tonal shifts in order to suggest the passage of light. This submovement of cubism often incorporated letters and sometimes entire words into the compositions, usually not for the subject of the words but for their design.[16]

This particular drawing, Picasso's *Nude* or *Female Nude*, 1910, develops out of strictly horizontal and vertical lines, lines that intersect and repeat each other to provide a certain definition of the image but also to release the impression of many other possibilities for the image's form, an uncertainty that serves to establish the cubist rejection of tradition, of mimesis, and most particularly, of the status quo. There are occasional short curved lines and a couple of diagonals, but the rest of the figure grows out of the shading carefully attached to the structural lines. Possibly, by looking carefully at the stance of the figure, one could determine its human origin, but that would be unlikely. The drawing's title is the main clue.[17]

As this figure zig-zags down the near-center of the paper, it evokes an impression of movement, both through the seeming shadow of the nodding of the "head" and the effort on the part of the viewer to make the figure sit down or stand up. The doubled exposure of the woman's rear leaves her in that awkwardly suspended posture halfway between the seated and the standing figure. The tension created here is produced by the flickering images of cubism's forte, the stop-and-go action seen under a strobe light's intermittent revelation and denial. The repeated patterning of the lines enforces the repetitive nature of the cubist technique: we want to select one set of lines to indicate the figure; the repeated lines reject our efforts to "delineate," to narrate the scene.[18]

Pablo Picasso (1881–1973). *Nude*, 1910. Charcoal. The Metropolitan Museum of Art: The Alfred Stieglitz Collection, 1949 (Photo: The Metropolitan Museum of Art). © ARS.

Current critics see this repetition as an indication of the breakdown of classical ideas of perspective. Goulding says that "the perspective [of cubist paintings], rather than being convergent [to a far focal point] is actually divergent," so that the cubist painting refuses to coalesce into the traditionally accepted perspectival point within the sphere of the canvas and instead creates a perspective that, while never nonexistent, spins outward, beyond the confines of the work.[19] Goulding believes that this type of perspective "[emphasizes] the 'materiality' of space" because it makes it "easier to fuse figure and surroundings."[20]

Bram Dijkstra, too, sees space as something material in cubism. He thinks that the cubists "make the space surrounding their objects in their paintings tangible, visible, and active by forcing it into geometric planes."[21] Dijkstra also thinks that the disruption of traditional perspective forced a disjunction of time as well as space in cubism: "Time . . . was a factor dulling the perceptions, and should be thwarted by crowding as much visual experience as possible within the moment of perception represented by the painting."[22] What critics such as Dijkstra seem to be responding to is the belief that artists and their audience of the early twentieth century were bored with realism, with conventional notions of perspective, of color, of composition, and so had to develop and entertain styles that would play with these forms to invigorate the original intentions of the forms, which had been and continued to be to represent reality but which now had to take into account a different reality.

There is seemingly no foreground or background in this drawing of Picasso's. The nude appears to be suspended in space just as she is suspended in movement. There is no ground to support her, nor are there identifying features to place her in a perspectival grid. Yet, the grid remains, transplanted from the traditional logic of single-point perspective (which has by now been disavowed) to the figure itself. It is as if the figure has become the seat of a new perspective, rootless in space and untied to horizon. The figure itself has been ruptured in the same way that the tradition of perspective disrupted the unstructured view of nature; the grid breaks down the human body into regular planes and straight lines. The voluptuousness of a nude woman has dissolved into the rigidity of the shadows and slashes of this new perspective.

Just as he effectively destroys accepted notions of realism by destroying the perspective grid, Picasso disrupts traditional notions of the movement of light through the picture plane by playing with the positions of light and dark. He directs himself more to patterns of light and dark, to the compositional effects of shading and line, than to the actual passage of light through his depicted scene. The effect of this play of light and dark is to fragment the image through a process of refraction.[23] The shadows tend to be where they should be for academic drawings: darker as the curve of the thigh, for instance, recedes in either direction from its uppermost, most reflective, surface. Almost invariably, these shadows run fairly evenly along the edge of one of the darkly drawn straight lines. However, the shaded areas do not always conform to standard practice. While the shading along the lower thigh is characteristic of traditional style (along the lower, almost seated portion of the upper leg), the upper thigh is heavily darkened along its rearmost length, emphasizing a triangle that does not correspond to normal human anatomy, as if Picasso were poking fun at the jutting out of this woman's rear end.

Because of this emphasis on light and dark and these repeated overlapping lines, as opposed to mimesis, there has been a lot of attention, both by critics contemporary to cubism and by current critics, to cubist notions of perspective and how they relate to views of time and space. The point of painting for the cubists was to flatten out the subject so that time and space are captured within the flatness of the canvas. Cubist painting spread out the three-dimensional object so that all of its aspects were present at one time. Early critics of the cubists focused on what they referred to as "harmony" and "rhythms" in the cubist work, partly because the cubists sapped their palettes of the excessive colors of their predecessors. Marius De Zayas, for instance, said of Picasso's work that "in his paintings perspective does not exist; in them there are nothing but harmonies suggested by form, and registers which succeed themselves to compose a general harmony which fills the rectangle that constitutes the picture."[24] The sense of the repetitive nature of the fragments, of the snippets of geometrical form of the cubist painting, denotes the cubist effort to break up narrative, the bourgeois force of convention.

The other major cubist artist, whose work was also represented in the Armory Show, is Georges Braque. His version of the cubist style is directly connected to the influence on him by Cezanne and is perhaps less academically inclined than Picasso's work. As is already apparent in Braque's fauve stage, his fragmentation of landscapes into geometric forms presaged his involvement in the later movement. His *Violin and*

Handbill, or *L'Affiche de Kubelick* of 1912, is an example of the radical nature of cubism when it adhered most seriously to its goals of abstraction and the presentation of all sides of a three-dimensional object at once. In such a reliance on compression of time and space, Braque crushes perspective and creates a canvas that no longer adheres to traditional methods of narrative.

This painting is like a drawing in that the artist applied straight and heavy lines of paint mostly on the horizontal or the vertical to render the subject by mimicking the action of charcoal while at the same time breaking up the space and disabling the audience's attempts to reconfigure the fragmentary composition. The heavy lines have shading on either side of them in greens and browns of varying tints. Generally speaking, if the paint is dark on one side of a line, it lightens as it moves across space to another line, and it will often be lighter on the other side of the second line.

What is unusual about this shading, however, is the extent to which the artist "worked" the paint in the so-called flat areas of the canvas. Instead of applying a uniform color to the small fields created by the heavy outlines, and instead of making a smooth transition from light to dark, Braque mixed the colors directly on the canvas so that they did not merge into one another completely. He also juxtaposed two different colors in various places in order to create sharp contrasts.

As with the rest of the adherents to the cubist movement, Braque restricts himself to a muted and limited palette in this painting.[25] The only colors here are white, black, and the mustard yellow of ocher, and various mixtures of the three, which serve to reinforce the refracted aspects of the images. The sole exception to this drabness is a sudden explosion of rose in the upper right corner of the canvas. This burst of warmth draws the viewer's eye partly because of the appealing quality of the hue, but partly also because this corner is the site of the graphic, of the words "Mozart" and "Kubelick."[26]

The sweep of the composition embodies a movement from the lower left of the canvas up to these words. A nearly continuous diagonal line propels this sweep with a vigor that cuts through the interjections of the opposing shapes. Below the words lies the apparent shape of a violin, though it could just as easily be a response to one of Raymond Duchamp-Villon's horses, with the end of the violin curling into the shape of a horse's nose. The muted colors of the violin, supported by that sharp diagonal, serve to support the warmer color of the upper right corner, so that the rest of the painting is reduced to a secondary position: it merely exists to buttress the eruption of the graphic onto the sphere of the painting.

This emphasis on the graphic prevents the painting from retaining a narrative focus. The words themselves mean little. We try, nevertheless, to reconstitute the work through these words, through the painting's title, through the scant image of the violin tuners. We want to see the poster advertising Jan Kubelick's violin performance. Neither the words nor the image take on narrative significance for us, though, through the weakened palette and compressed perspective of the image and the lack of context for the words, a similar treatment that Moore provides for the nectarine in her cubist effort.

"Nine Nectarines" is a near-exact rendering of one of Picasso's cubist still lifes. Picasso and Braque destroyed the traditional standards of perspective by presenting table tops askew, fruit wildly lopsided, and wall surfaces completely distorted. In other words, by showing more than one perspective plane at a time, these painters changed techniques of representation and denied narrative continuity through the standard one-point perspective. They also, in the cubist frame of mind, tried to present scenes simultaneously from as many points of view as possible. Picasso's *Fruit Bowl*, for instance, while not yet in his major cubist style, still flattens the fruit into random, nearly unrecognizable shapes and gives the impression of allowing us to see all of the fruit in the bowl at once, a normal impossibility. The bowl that the fruit sits in extends much further to the left of the canvas than to the right, belying its true rounded, regular form. The surface that the bowl sits on is on the same plane as the wall. Only a drawn line and color shift indicate where the table stops and the wall starts. The tonal changes give no indication of light source or direction.

Moore's "Nine Nectarines" also presents the all-around view of her fruit by means of an associative technique that breaks down perspectival tradition in much the same way that Picasso did.[27] Moore begins the poem by describing the fruits:

> Fuzzless through slender crescent leaves
> of green or blue or
> both, in the Chinese style, the four

> pairs' half-moon leaf-mosaic turns
> out to the sun the sprinkled blush
> of puce-American-Beauty pink
> applied to bees-wax gray by the
> uninquiring brush
> of mercantile bookbinding.
>
> (CP 29)

These fruits are ripening on a branch of their tree. This very description is cubist in nature: the "leaf-mosaic" of "green or blue or / both" that gives the impression of fractured light; the "slender crescent leaves" that slash through the air in arcs similar to those in Picasso's cubist drawing, carving the ground into ruptured perspective; and the merest hint of "blush" that has been added to the overall "bees-wax gray" of the cubist palette.

This description of the fruits, which involves their color, texture, and already the associations of an art, that of bookbinding, begins the train of thought that will compel the poet to wander from the fruit itself, the inspiration for this poem, to other scarcely connected impressions. This wandering about takes us in the same direction that the cubist painter does: toward a disruption of perspective and a turn away from narrative. The cubist's flickering images, which float in an unfocused, groundless field, periodically come into high relief so that we can connect the pieces of the puzzle, as it were, to decipher the represented subject. In the same way, the seeming movement away from her topic allows Moore to skip to other moments of crystalline clarity, the pieces of which she leaves for us to combine in a coherent order.

At first these nectarines make her think of other related fruits that are even more exotic: "the peach *Yu*," "the Italian / peach-nut," the "Persian plum," and the "Ispahan / secluded wall-grown nectarine." They also make her ponder the possible origins of the peach relative: "found in China first. But was it wild?" The varieties of the fruit and its history are additional methods of the poet's efforts to represent them in their entirety and are examples of the ultimately greater flexibility of the verbal form of cubism.

Moore's eye moves back to the nectarines for a moment and admires their perfections—they look perfect—but then she retreats entirely from the fruit to wander in her imagination to other artifacts brought to her mind through musings, reinforcing the disconnections between the images of the poem, degenerating the narrative through a compression of perspective. She thinks of the moose (or is it a horse, or an ass?) that appears on a plate of hers.

The poem then breaks off entirely with a series of dots across the page, disrupting any continuity that might have been left in the poem, severing connections that serve to sustain narrative. When the poem resumes, it is with her feeling that the Chinese would understand the nectarine the best because it originated in their country. Moore looks at a piece of Chinese porcelain while she considers this possibility, one which portrays the Chinese unicorn that loved to eat nectarines. The poem ends with, "It was a Chinese who imagined this masterpiece," leaving us with the impression that the artist's imagination shapes the work around the subject so that the product is a mingling of the reality of what is seen and the irreality of what is created internally by the artist.

Though she writes in her essay "Subject, Predicate, Object" that "the objective [of poetry] is architecture, never demolition," in her work Moore adheres to Picasso's view of cubism as a "horde of destructions," the destruction primarily of traditional narrative through compressed perspective.[28] Cubist techniques of condensed perspective appear in Moore's work in such poems as "Nine Nectarines," in which she flattens out time, as it were, to offer the present nectarines—as well as their history and their future—within the compass of the one poem read at an instant, unrestricted by the nectarines' appearance alone.

The wanderings of Moore's mind as she contemplates the fruit on its branches reflect the all-around view of the cubist. Not only does she show us the fruit, she talks of other, similar fruit, of the fruit's origins, and of related artifacts of memory that the fruit calls to her mind. We see, then, all around the nectarine, not just how it looks but the essence of nectarineness in a figurative sense. Moore tells us all there is to know about it without relying on the logic of perspective but insisting instead on the fragmented notions of the cubist and the associative thinker through a denial of standards of perspective. What she portrays is shattered by the apparent randomness of her thought, leaving the work of reconstruction to the audience.

As became apparent in my discussion of Braque's cubist painting, the early cubists reduced their palettes to a minimum, thereby enhancing their treatment of lights and darks and refracting the passage of light within the canvas. The cubists reacted against the fauve palette and opted for a more restricted, more muted range of grays, blues, and browns. No longer is color the transmitter of emotion; it becomes instead the cubist emblem for the rejection of representation as a direct adherent to nature, to mimesis. The early cubist champion Alfred Barr sees the cubist palette as a direct response to the movement's disruption of form. He says that analytical cubism is so termed because of a "progressive tearing apart or disintegrating of natural forms. During this progression, color was gradually eliminated."[29] The muted and contained quality of cubist color violates the bourgeois sense of reality, yet, at the same time, it responds to the culture's fear of the vibrant.

The cubist palette is directly related to the artist's sense of light. The passage of light through the canvas is no longer defined by the direct influence of the light falling from a window and hitting surfaces in an interior, as in a Vermeer or Velasquez, nor is it the light filtered through the leaves of a garden onto water, as in an impressionist work. Now the artists wanted to recreate the patterns of light and dark without reference to an actual light source. Picasso, for instance, developed his image through the use of darks and lights, with tints rather than hues. He wanted shadows to bear the same relevance within the composition as the highlights—shadows became merely another shape in the cubist work. They no longer necessarily indicate the development of the illusion in two dimensions of a three-dimensional object, scene or figure, but in fact serve to subvert that original function of *chiaroscuro*. De Zayas says of the cubist in *Camera Work*: "To him color does not exist, but only the effects of light. This produces in matter certain vibrations, which produce in the individual certain impressions."[30] These vibrations of light fracture traditional light patterns and set up a shimmering refraction, again disrupting narrative by breaking up the light on an image, and therefore the image itself, into myriad fragments.

Not only did the cubists remove prismatic colors from their work, they broke the previously important color fields down into mosaics of light and dark patterns. Clement Greenberg, in his seminal essay on collage, reasoned that for the cubists, "light and dark . . . had begun to act more immediately as cadences of design rather than as plastic description or definition."[31] In order to enhance this "design" aspect of painting, the cubists had to mute their palettes because the emphasis on light versus dark took precedence over color. This palette reduction had the paradoxical effect of allowing a more complete fracture of the passage of light on the canvas.

The breakup of the canvas into lights and darks, a refraction of typical light patterns, also appears in Moore's poetry through the faceted treatment of indistinct images.[32] An example of cubistic prismatic effects appears in "The Fish."[33] The early version of this poem appeared in *The Egoist* magazine in 1918.[34] Its form in Moore's *Observations* (1924) is significantly different from its earlier version. When revising her work for the later edition of her poems, Moore changed the lengths of the first and second lines of each stanza in order to eliminate most internal rhymes, making the poem less cubistic. For example, the first line of the 1918 poem reads, "Wade through black jade." Moore changed this line for the later version to read: "Wade / through black jade" (O 43). These changes in the poem diminish the tightening force of the interior rhyme, which she reused in the third lines of each stanza, "side" rhyming with "hide," "Ness" with "crevices," and so on.

Reducing the ability of the ends of the lines to bounce off their beginnings mitigates the cubistic effects of the rest of the poem. In spite of that, the mosaic of images created by the broken lines operates as a prism, disrupting narrative connectives between each image. The action of the poem mimics the action of the sea and the fish within it by presenting shimmering glimpses of shapes under the water, the "crow-blue mussel-shells," the "submerged shafts of the / sun," and the "crabs like / green / lilies and submarine / toadstools" (O 43).[35] The vibrant colors and distinctive shapes of the undersea scene flicker in and out of sight as the poet traces the movement of the fish and the water without a particular sense of progression. It is the lack of logical goals or of advancement, the seemingly random juxtaposition of unrelated elements, that creates a sense of simultaneity in this poem by disrupting the time continuum of narration and replacing it with a scene that is ostensibly available all at once. In this poem, in fact, simultaneity and cubism merge, one through the time distortion, the other through the faceting of an image. As in cubist paintings, there is no distinction in "The Fish" between the figure and the ground—they are compressed and merged.

At the same time, however, Moore felt compelled to end the poem in the ostensibly traditional manner of an ethical statement: "Repeated / evidence has proved that it can / live / on what cannot revive / its youth. The sea grows old in it" (O 44). I call this stanza "ostensibly conclusive" because it has the tenor and language of the pragmatic statement of conclusion with moral overtones. But the line has no referent. The "Repeated / evidence has proved" has the sound of a scientific discussion, if not of an advertisement claiming a scientific validity, giving the beginning of the sentence an empirically based, and therefore rational and believable feel. However, the "it" in both of the last sentences is difficult to place.[36] It could refer to the chasm side of the cliff, to the evidence, to the sea, or to any number of the images that Moore has brought into the body of the poem.

By leaving the end of the poem suspended, Moore stresses an imagistic view of the sea, with its colors and shapes, and abandons the moralistic tone of the parable, allowing the simultaneous effects of the cubist techniques of the poem to take precedence over tradition.[37] Her treatment of the undersea scene, as if seen through the refraction of moving water, takes on the antinarrative of cubism by creating disjunctures between the elements of the ocean.

Another antinarrative technique that the cubists adopted is repetition with variations, a method through which they could induce change in the monolithic bourgeois culture. Kirk Varnedoe, in his *A Fine Disregard: What Makes Modern Art Modern*, sees repetition as a major hallmark of the modernism movement: "Fragmentation and repetition are metaphors of modernity, in its unresolved complexity. On the one hand, the thing [is] ripped from its former integral context, and given independent life, as indicative of the disruptions of new individual freedom, and on the other, the form recur[s] in exact or near-exact identity as indicative of new conceptions of collective order."[38] Varnedoe's idea that repetition shows the effects of "new conceptions of collective order" harkens back to Adorno's idea that technical innovations signal breaks from the old culture. By repeating something, but something that has been transmuted, that has evolved somewhat, the artist can show that the repetitions rely on the old institutions, but the variations are the changes that the artist sees happening, or wants to see happening.

Gertrude Stein's prose is a prime example of how repetition can work on the level of grammar. The repetitions with variations in Stein's prose, in her portraits of Picasso and Matisse as well as in *Tender Buttons*, were the main technical method she used to express the dynamics of cubism. For example, Stein's 1909 portrait of Picasso begins: "One whom some were certainly following was one who was completely charming. One whom some were certainly following was one who was charming. One whom some were following was one who was completely charming. One whom some were following was one who was certainly completely charming."[39] Each sentence represents a facet of the prismatically fragmented cubist portrait. Each variation develops a new facet, so that over the course of an entire segment of a Stein portrait she has presented her subject from all sides. In this case, she suggests the strength of Picasso's personality and his ability to draw people to him by repeating "charming" several times over. By reducing grammatical sections into repeated sections, the cumulative effect of Stein's portrait of Picasso is to define Picasso's personality and ability.

Here, too, the reader must fill in the gaps between the splintered clauses in order to create a whole view of her subject. Stein never describes Picasso in the straightforward manner of the realists; she circles around his personality and his abilities in an attempt to present not just his looks or his actions but his essence, as the cubists did in their portraits. And she is a cubist artist not just in her faceting of the subject but also in her treatment of time. By figuratively opening up the three-dimensional view of Picasso so that he can be seen in the round on a two-dimensional plane, Stein tried to compress time into the instant; the temporally disjunctive image of Picasso is available all at once.

Wendy Steiner contends that the "abstract elements of grammar" in writing correspond to the abstract elements of "geometry" in cubistic painting.[40] Stein subverts the accepted role of "nouns, verbs, adjectives and adverbs" that, according to Steiner, "like the icons of synthetic cubism, are arranged in nonrepresentational patterns."[41] Literary cubists, by placing words in positions that vitiate their traditional grammatical functions, shatter our ability to decipher the meanings of these words and the references of their sentences. Steiner compares the small, planar, nonrepresentational units of cubism to "syncategorematic words, shifters, or 'pronouns' [Jakobson's word]."

In these relations that Steiner draws, however, she fails to take into account the vibration that remains in a word that has been removed from its context—a verb that has been divorced from its active position, that has been stripped of its transitive role, yet resonates with the shadows of its verbness. Steiner also overlooks the sensuality of painting as opposed to literature. An abstract painting, of a Jackson Pollack for instance, has depth, texture, and color, all of which are absent from abstract literature.

Painting can never really be abstract, then; it must always stimulate our symbolizing tendencies. Nonrepresentational painting always represents something through its sensual character. In the same way, though they are not sensual, words always retain their "symbolic" meaning.

Like the cubists, then, Stein attempted to abstract time, although, also like the visual artists, she remained timebound because the only way to capture the moment is through particulars. Because written language is experienced line by line or through syntactical units, the reader can never escape the linear progression of time. In this sense, the visual arts were more adept at time compression than were the written ones.

The cubist techniques of the nonexpatriate American poets took a different course from that of Stein. Instead of jumbling standard word order in order to drain the words of their meanings, the other Americans relied on the prismatic effects of the juxtaposition of snipped images. Their view of cubism rests more on their interest in the fragmented picture and in representing it in concise language than on Stein's technique of presenting the shallowness that the whole must be if it is to be contained in one sentence.[42] Both Stein and Moore use repetition to create works allied to the cubist movement, but each takes a distinct route to it. Stein's prose is cubist on the level of grammar, while Moore's is cubist on the level of the image.

Moore's "Those Various Scalpels" is a portrait that uses the same techniques of cubist representation as Stein. Who this person is that Moore is depicting is in question; in some respects, its very identity is effaced by the scrambling poetic technique of the cubist.[43] By reinscribing the figure through the repetition of the type that I refer to in my discussion of Picasso's drawing, Moore translates visual forms into verbal ones. In recasting the pictorial line, she repeats details of the figure, each time with increased and more outflung metaphor. Her first mention of an image or object is conventional and objective, mirroring the standard cultural view of mimesis. The subsequent impression or impressions of these images become much more farflung, revealing the work of the imagination to strain the borders of conventionality, to revise the status quo in the same way that she is "revising" the image.

Each item in the poem is named and then renamed, beginning with the title. "Those Various Scalpels" sets up the topic of the poem, with its interest in dissection, but scalpels is renamed with "those / various sounds," a reconfiguration of a dissecting or operating instrument that makes no logical sense. This logic disjunction sets up a break from the staid rationality of the bourgeoisie. These "sounds" are repeated again here with "intermingled / echoes / struck from thin glasses successively at random," a poetic, and therefore imaginatively inspired, rendering of the thinly sharp sounds of the instruments rattling together (O 61).[44] Moore enhances this feel of these sounds with her hissing tones from "consistently indistinct" and "glasses successively."

The next overtly named image is "your hair."[45] First, the poet elaborates on mere hair by saying that it is like "the tails of two / fighting-cocks head to head in stone," an unlikely non sequitor that recreates the odd sweep of the hair but is anticonventional in its display of illogic and in its representation of hair beyond the realm of the normative. Moore presses this exaggeration in her second reference to hair: "like sculptured / scimitars re- / peating the curve of your ears in reverse order" (O 61). Again, this image of curved swords replicates the upward movement of the hair, but like the hair shaped like rooster tails, the conjunction of hair with sabers from an exotic source stretches the action of logic beyond its abilities. The ostensible topic here is hair, but its real topic is disruption of the "outline" of the image by redescribing it with increasingly elaborate comparisons to take it out of the mundaneness of its unimaginative culture.

The third image works in much the same manner but with only one repetition: "your eyes" is replaced only by "flowers of ice / / and / snow / sown by tearing winds on the cordage of disabled / ships" (O 61). The stretch of this repetition away from its original feature, however, makes up for its singularity. The extreme of the compound metaphor of flowers that grow out of some medium and dire storm situations on ships at sea snaps the illusory logic of the poem into the control of the imagination, that anti-status-quo force that pulls the poem out of the narrative continuum.

The oddness of the next two repetitions continues the operation of the cubist enterprise to reject narration. "Your raised hand" becomes "an ambiguous signature." Signature has varied meanings, one of which is a mark of some kind to indicate identity.[46] The "ambiguity" of identity created by the lifted hand undermines the concrete certainty of "signature," removing the definitive character of the "outline" of the name.

The sureness of the name "your cheeks," too, is erased through the variation that follows it. Instead of merely stating that the cheeks of the figurine are red, Moore relates their color to "those rosettes / of blood on the stone floors of French châteaux, with / regard to which the guides are so affirmative" (O 61). While she does not use the word ambiguity here, Moore sets up an ambiguous situation by leaving open the reference to actual blood (the story about which may be apocryphal, but the tour guides are definite about it) or to a pattern on the stone floor that resembles roses. This double possibility traces the double line of the figure's cheeks, mimicking the repeated line of the cubist drawing that allows us to "see" the figure while at the same time destroying it.

The next repetition begins with "your other hand," but it does not repeat the hand exactly—instead it refers to what is in the hand: "a / bundle of lances," those scalpels that started the poem. There is, however, the customary confusion about these lances. They appear, illlogically, to become the "collection of half a dozen little objects," the jewels and the fruit, "tied with silver" (O 61–62). The confusion induced by the intentionally elusive syntax recreates the escape from narrative engaged in by the cubist painters.

The last repetition in this poem refers to the figure's dress, "a magnificent square / cathedral tower of uniform / and at the same time diverse appearance" (O 62). The idea that the dress could be a tower, clothing as architecture, is improbable but possible, given the stylistic variations on figuration in the Renaissance. This odd connection is overwhelmed, though, by the "uniform / and at the same time diverse appearance." In some ways the paradox that this statement reveals is the same paradox facing modern writers and artists such as Moore: the uniformity is the expression of conformity that they adhere to in their reliance on conventional subjects; the diversity is their desire to break free of conventionality.

Moore reinforces this inner turmoil more explicitly in her following repetition of the dress: "a species of / vertical vineyard rustling in the storm / of conventional opinion" (O 62). Suddenly this figure represents to her a force against the bourgeoisie, and it is perhaps in these more oblique repetitions that Moore has been building this case. Certainly, the bizarre image of the dress as a "vertical vineyard" confutes the rational and moral base of the dominant culture. Its very oddness is a rebellion, but the image itself is of Moore's imagination, revealing that the rebellion is not seated in the image of the figure but in Moore herself.

"Are they weapons or scalpels?" refers back to the lances in the figure's hand, but they are there to address "conventional opinion," either to destroy it because it is ultimately too repressive or to dissect it to comprehend its underlying operations. Moore thinks these are ideal "instruments" for this purpose, but she ends the poem with an oblique question in her fear of being too obviously hostile to her own adherence to the status quo: "Why dissect destiny with instruments / which / are more highly specialized than the tissues of destiny itself?" (O 62). These weapons against the overwhelmingly repressive culture are in fact too "sophisticated" to bother with such an archaic system; the features of culture, that which determines and forces upon us our destiny, are too obvious, and I think in the end, too strong, for these sharp little knives of criticism that Moore levels at them.

By first laying out each image of this poem in a strictly conventional and matter-of-fact manner, Moore displays her allegiance to and her sense of conformity to her culture. This first naming of the features of the figure is the equivalent to the clear single line denoting the outline of the traditional drawing. However, by renaming each image at least once and in quick succession, and with the heightened expanse of flamboyant description and metaphor, she intensifies her dislike of that culture and re-creates a new one, one driven by the imagination rather than by the mundaneness of submission to the petit bourgeoisie. The superimposition of the recreated image over the traditional one also reenacts the same technique that the cubist draughtsman used in layering lines to signify the outline and shape of a figure, but to refuse to denote that figure clearly, to retain other possibilities for the figure's shape, movement, and identity.

Moore's poetry follows cubist practice in its disruption of perspectival convention, in its antinarrative quality, in its sense of composition that negates the central focus of the academics. By fragmenting her subjects, by relying on principles of repetition, and by altering conventional ideas of time and space, Moore re-creates in poetry the same formal techniques that the cubists invented for the visual arts. Like the cubists, then, Moore uses shading and faceting to depict her subject, and like the collage artists, as I will show in the next chapter, she uses quotation to disrupt traditional narrative movement.

3
"Anthology of Words": Marianne Moore's Collage

Marianne Moore kept a scrapbook during the 1910s that overlapped with the New York Armory Show, an exhibition that introduced Americans to contemporary European art from the postimpressionists to the cubists. She clipped six articles on the show for her scrapbook. These articles compose a semicollage of the response to the show by presenting quotations from various critics with little or no introduction. Moore expresses her affinity to collage not only by this simple collection of articles about the cubist artists but also by her reshaping of these articles, her cutting out, rearranging, and altering them. There was no work of collage in the Armory Show because Picasso was just making his first one, *Still Life with Chair Caning*, in 1912, when the show's curators were formulating the exhibition, but the impetus to develop collage techniques was apparent already in the cubist formulation. Moore reveals the influence of the visual arts not only through her scrapbook but through her use of collage in her poetry, especially in "Marriage" and "An Octopus."

The opinions of the authors in Moore's collage, this scrapbook on the Armory Show, range from the fascinated and explanatory to the outraged and declamatory. One of the pieces that Moore saved for her book was a paragraph of an article written by Theodore Roosevelt.[1] Roosevelt was scandalized by the art in the show. In this paragraph, pasted over a picture from another article, he compared Duchamp's *Nude Descending a Staircase* to the Navajo rug in his bathroom, "which on any proper interpretation of the Cubist theory, is a far more satisfactory and decorative picture."[2] Roosevelt viewed the primitive movement in the contemporary arts as "a smirking pose of retrogression."[3] However, because Moore kept only the paragraph of Roosevelt's article on the Navajo rug, and because she decontextualized it by placing it in the middle of an article on an entirely different subject, she diminished the impact of its negative sentiment, and, in fact, this gesture of formal realignment of a "retrograde" content is a clear parallel to Moore's radical poetic technique.

The other articles that Moore saved were written by critics more sensitive to the endeavors of the avant-garde artists, demonstrating Moore's sympathy for their work. She must have received at home, or have been given by friends, two journals: *Current Opinion* and *The Literary Digest*. Both of these magazines were along the lines of our *Newsweek* or *Time*, fairly bland but comprehensive distributors of current events and other general news of the arts and sciences. Of the remaining five articles, four were composed of quoted material from other sources gathered together by anonymous critics. John Quinn, who bought several works in the Armory Show, is represented here, as are the photographer and avant-garde gallery owner Alfred Stieglitz and the critics J. Nilsen Laurvik, Charles Caffin, and James Gregg. Both Caffin and Laurvik also wrote pieces for Stieglitz's journal *Camera Work*.

A section of an article from *Current Opinion* includes brief reviews of the Armory Show from differing but generally favorable points of view.[4] "Bedlam in Art" concludes that "cubism has merely carried the thing [abstraction] to its logical conclusion." "Post-Impressionism Outgrown" begins with Harriet Monroe's scandalized opinion of Matisse's work—"The most hideous monstrosities ever perpetuated in the name of long-suffering art"—but ends with a quick review of other critics who give the early-twentieth-century art more "serious consideration." "Art Madness Recaptured" includes a quotation from Marlowe—"a fine madness"—to describe avant-garde innovations, and Caffin's contribution to "Matisse and Picabia Compared" relates the "real sensation of the spiritual impressiveness of the scene." These articles, then, tend to express appreciation of innovations in the early-twentieth-century visual arts, indicating not only Moore's interest in them but also their influence on her.

Of all pictorial modes, collage is possibly the most political and the most subtly subversive. Violating conventional rules about esthetic correctness and cohesiveness through the juxtaposition of disparate materials, collage registers its critique of the status quo at the level of technique itself. Because of its interartistic transgressiveness, collage is also the visual form most amenable for approximation by verbal artists. It is therefore not surprising to see collage as a central component of the iconoclastic poetic manifestos in the early decades of this century. Although the names that usually come to mind in this respect are Ezra Pound and T. S. Eliot, a prominent place must also be given to Marianne Moore. Indeed, it could be argued that Moore was more politically perceptive than either of her male counterparts, for she used collage to question that most entrenched of all bourgeois institutions—namely, marriage.

Moore's use of collage techniques in her poetry has not gone unnoticed; nor—given that her most ambitious poem is entitled "Marriage"—has her concern with this subject been overlooked.[5] What remains to be explored, however, is the way in which these two facets work together, or the way in which Moore's affinities with collage are not limited to its

Pablo Picasso (1881–1973). *Still Life with Chair Caning*, 1912. Oil and coated oil cloth, $10\frac{5}{8}$ X $13\frac{3}{4}$ in. Musée Picasso, Paris (Photo: Musée Picasso). © ARS.

technical innovations but extend to its subversive political agenda as well.

By addressing Moore's practice in this way, I will also be implicitly challenging the current view that discussions of interart relationships must not be based on shared "content" but instead should confine themselves to matters of how one art form "converts" the techniques of another.[6] Pretending to respect the "other," such arguments may reflect just how much bourgeois notions of marriage continue to inform current critical theory and practice.

Collage first appeared in the visual arts when Pablo Picasso and Georges Braque, concurrently, began to affix to their canvasses recognizable articles from daily life. Painting thus became less a "fabrication" in the traditional sense and more an interaction between the artist's imagination (i.e., esthetic operations) and external objects and influences. The first collage in the visual arts was constructed by Picasso in May 1912. Entitled *Still Life with Chair Caning*, it takes the form of a horizontally positioned oval surrounded by rope.[7] The main feature of this collage is a large piece of oilcloth in the lower left quadrant that has printed on it a trompe l'oeil representation of chair caning. Although at this stage Picasso did not use actual newspaper clippings, this recourse to the verbal is present in the form of the letters "JOU," suggesting *Le Journal,* which he painted directly on the canvas. "JOU" sets up a continual reverberation between the practical function of a newspaper and the notion of the "play" involved in the act of incorporating such material. The "caning" sets up the same type of play between its pretense of texture and source and the actual nature and role of such material.

The later and more radical collagists had two predominant purposes in employing the collage techniques developed by Picasso and Braque: *épater les bourgeoisie* and to reject traditions of mimesis.[8] According to critics interested in the political ramifications of radical art techniques, such as Peter Bürger, Patricia Leighton, and Clement Greenberg, the avant-garde (among them the collagists and all the formalists, but in particular the dadaists) stood in an "adversary relationship to bourgeois culture."[9] Although the subversive quality of the dada arts perhaps had its original source in the fears of total apocalypse brought on by the First World War, by the 1920s it became a total disavowal of the social order. According to Marc Dachy, "for the old forms invested with social authority void now of any content [the dadaists] substituted new, shifting transient, unfinished forms. . . . There was a negation of culture."[10] The dadaists thus rejected culture by undermining the notion of established forms, their formal innovations allowing a denial of cultural tradition.

The radical forms that the dadaists adopted also refuted the norms of mimesis and representation by subverting notions of perspective that had developed during the Renaissance. Marjorie Perloff has argued that collage challenges "the fundamental principle of Western painting . . . that a picture is a window on reality, an imaginary transparency through which an illusion is discerned. Collage also subverts all conventional figure-ground relationships."[11] In the same way, "a fundamental principle" of Western culture is that marriage is a "reality" and that all individuals need to be viewed in terms of this "figure-ground relationship."

The dadaists were the most radical in their uses of collage techniques because they were the strongest in their rejection of bourgeois values and the most interested in relations between the visual arts and the written ones. Marcel Duchamp described the dada movement in 1946 by saying that it "was intimately and consciously involved with 'literature.'. . . It was a way to get out of a state of mind—to avoid being influenced by one's immediate environment, or by the past."[12] In the same way the poets of the time reached out to methods of the visual arts to reassess restrictions of their own culture and to investigate possible alternatives.

Collage allowed the poets of the early twentieth century to establish a new relationship between the act of imagination and the resultant view of reality. Just as notions of perspective change, definitions of reality and of how a culture approached it had to adjust. According to Jacob Korg, "collage juxtaposes unprocessed reality with the product of the artist's imagination, exhibiting the radical heterogeneity of the actual and the conceptual, and exploiting the contrast between them."[13] Korg goes on to observe that "the literary equivalent of the painter's collage is . . . quotation—not conventional quotation, but the kind that represents itself as an interpolation, interrupting the text, and even conflicting with the writer's purposes, as if it were an eruption of raw reality."[14] While Korg is discussing collage in light of Ezra Pound's poetry, I believe that his definition works well with Moore's own style. Like Pound, Moore brought quotations into her work repeatedly, in a poetic reenactment of the *papiers collés* of the European visual artists.

In her poetry Moore draws upon factual data from her reading, from her memory, and from history. Such allusions give her poems a multifaceted depth, as in her meditation in "Nine Nectarines" in which she thinks of the fruit's Chinese origins. They add an exotic flavor to "Those Various Scalpels," in which she mentions "the stone floors of French châteaux," the "emeralds from / Persia / and the fractional magnificence of Florentine / goldwork" (O 61). Moore's "pack rat" method of using the fund of history and memory as her poetic sources, especially through her continual retrieval of quotations and facts from multifarious sources that she brings together out of context into the newly formed context of her poem, resembles the way the cubist painter took items such as pieces of wood, rope, or caning from their original settings and placed them in the newly created setting of the painting, changing their meanings yet always allowing referral back to their origins. Similarly, just as collage utilized mundane objects, so Moore's quotations are drawn not only from classical sources; they can be as impersonal as the guide to the National Park Services, which she used for "An Octopus," and as personal as overheard or remembered remarks by her friends and family.[15] Moreover, Moore often changes quotations from their original form before inserting them into her poems, just as Picasso or Braque would cut or tear his pieces of newspaper before placing them on the canvas.[16]

While Moore inserts quotations from other sources in most of her poetry, the most compelling examples of her use of such collage are "Marriage" and "An Octopus." These are her two longest poems, the closest she comes to the epic form so prevalent among the modernist poets. Moore's epics, however, have a feminist orientation; she relates social and cultural history through her analyses of the institution of marriage and Mount Rainier National Park instead of through a focus on public politics and national events. "Marriage" plays a particularly central role in Moore's oeuvre, mainly because its calculated efforts to question marriage as a viable social institution become a marked emblem of the essentially subversive character of her work.[17] As such, this poem is truly Moore's effort at a manifesto but is actually an antimanifesto in its criticism of the institution.[18]

"Marriage" begins with a general description of the institution in economic language. The poem then looks at the generic figures of the woman and man, at their gendered personalities. Once these figures have been established, a long discussion ensues between a male and a female character. It is generally backbiting and nasty, particularly on the part of the female speaker. The poem concludes with an overview of marriage, with highly convoluted language that indicates a type of retreat on Moore's part and her overall disappointment with the marital practice.

Moore's continued modesty about her work, especially this poem, and her obscure and teasingly unhelpful notes at the end of her *Complete Poems*, underplay the intensity with which she denigrates social behaviors, from marriage to war, as I have argued above. In an interview with Grace Schulman, for instance, Moore described "Marriage" as "just an anthology of words that I didn't want to lose, that I liked very much, and I put them together as plausibly as I could. So people daren't derive a whole philosophy of life from *that*."[19] In her quietly dismissive manner, Moore deflects attention away from the way the poem uses collage to criticize the marital institution.

Moore's disapproval of marriage is most obvious in her poetry notebook at the Rosenbach Museum and Library that shows her revisions and the process involved in her collection of materials, including her notes for "Marriage" and "An Octopus."[20] A careful analysis of the notebook suggests that a paradoxical doubleness characterizes her collage techniques. Her revisions of her own words tend to mute her disapproval of the marital conventions, while at the same time her revisions of quotations drawn from other sources tend to sharpen her critical stance toward marriage. Much of this critical aspect of her attitude toward marriage can be traced to her alliance with the dada movement, which had its strong followers in New York (Marcel Duchamp and Francis Picabia, among them) and which also involved iconoclasm and reclamation, as I will discuss further in the following chapter.

In "Marriage," Moore's recourse to materials from varied sources serves to fracture formal patterns traditionally associated with poetry and creates instead the rupturing effects of collage. If she had retained conventional poetic forms, she would have upheld the type of "social authority" that the collagists were attempting to overthrow. In her presentation of marriage, Moore is antilyrical and aphoristic. She undermines lyrical rhythms through the use of random syllabics—this poem is actually unlike her others in its lack of syllable patterning—and through juxtapositions of disparate ideas. The complexity of the dissociated thoughts thrown together in a seeming jumble dissolves the linguistic and thematic harmonies, harmonies that are so basic to the traditions of lyrical poetry. Technical disruptions, then, play into social subversion by severing formal connections with the traditions of the past.

In addition to the quotations that appear in "Marriage," the notebook at the Rosenbach museum includes early drafts of the poem itself.[21] These quotations suggest that if one of the roles of the poem is merely to define marriage, Moore's purpose is equally to undermine it.[22] Excluded from the final version of the poem, such remarks are openly critical of marriage. Clearly, Moore felt uncomfortable with expressing hostility directly and thus turned to methods of collage that would allow her to retain her disapproval of marriage while tempering the intensity of her feelings toward it.

A quotation in "Marriage" continues to bear the meaning it has in its original source, yet it also carries the new meaning it acquires by its position in the poem, by what surrounds it, by the tenor of the work in general, and by how the poet has cropped it. Moore reminds us of her quotations' original context by giving references, albeit vague, in the back of her *Complete Poems*. The overall intent of the quotation is then changed from its original one, adjusted in tone, as it were, by the nature of the rest of the poem. Moore thereby makes a new work of art and renews the tradition of marriage, as well, so that both marriage and poetic conventions can be reassessed for their current value.

Moore's poem is difficult to decipher because the reader has to make connections between seemingly random quotations. In this sense, "Marriage" reminds us of one of Duchamp's cubist-futurist paintings in the Armory Show. Just as he presents clear "splinters" of figures descending the stairs or waiting for a train, so Moore presents precise details and quotations. By interlacing these quotations with her own aphoristic statements, Moore mimics the spliced shapes of Duchamp's figures in motion. An understanding of "Marriage" requires the attempt to "see" all Moore's fragments at once, just as it requires attention to the reverberations between the original contexts of several quotations and their revised contexts in "Marriage."

Our understanding of these intentions is complicated by Moore's ambivalent feelings about the marital state. Although she believes firmly in the continued viability of the institution, as evidenced in her focus on it in this poem, she nevertheless also critiques it. Marriage tends to place men in power over women, denigrating women's capabilities. Moore ridicules male authority in this poem and makes other disparaging remarks about the social form, as a true dadaist, but she, however reluctantly, admits to its strength. This ambivalence appears in the cutting and shaping of Moore's quotations, as well as in the relationship between the quotations' old and new contexts.[23] Moore almost always changes her quotations when placing them in her poem, partly probably for esthetic reasons, partly, however, for argumentative reasons. Moore wants her quotations to bear certain highly refined intimations. In this sense Moore adapts to poetry the collage technique of *déchirage*, "to tear out roughly," as opposed to the technique of *découpage*, "to cut out neatly."

As Patricia Willis points out, Moore drew many of the quotations that she used in "Marriage" from Richard Baxter's *The Saint's Everlasting Rest*, a 1650 Calvinist prescription for passage to heaven.[24] Three of the quotations from Baxter's work that appear in the Rosenbach notebook are used in the poem to denigrate the marital state. Moore changed the Baxter quotations very little: "the speedy stream and waterfall which violently bears all before it" changes to "the industrious waterfall, / 'the speedy stream / which violently bears all before it'" (CP 64); Baxter's words—"seldom and cold, up and down, mixed and malarial with a good day and a bad"—remain the same in the poem (CP 66); and "perceiving a fire effectual to extinguish fire" becomes "'the illusion of a fire / effectual to extinguish fire'" (CP 65).

These phrases appear in the poem in various forms of criticism of marriage. When Adam begins to speak, his pedantic, ceaseless rambling is compared to the "stream / which violently bears all before it": nothing can stop him or make him shift his course. "Seldom and cold" follows "Married people often look that way" and gives married life a vast depth of ennui. Marriage, in fact, is a state that unmarried people desire as a panacea to their problems (the desire to be married is "'the illusion of a fire / effectual to extinguish fire'"), but it is an illusory desire that dwindles at the moment of entrance into the married state, a state that cannot satisfy desire.

Early in "Marriage," Moore incorporates the cynical language of Sir Francis Bacon: "'Of circular traditions and impostures, / committing many spoils'" (CP 62). As Margaret Holley has noted, Moore took this quotation from the *Encyclopedia Brittanica*: "I have taken all knowledge to be my province and if I could purge it of two sorts of errors, whereof the one with frivolous disputation, confutations and verbosities, the other with blind experiments and circular traditions and impostures hath committed so many spoils, I hope I shall bring in industrious observations."[25] Moore's pruning of Bacon's language suggests the way she shapes borrowed quotations to fit her needs. In this case, she changes Bacon's topic from knowledge to marriage. She also cuts out "frivolous disputation, confutations and verbosities" as well as "blind experiments," all of which would denigrate the importance of the marital state. What she leaves in, however, equally condemns marriage. Although "circular tradition" is ambiguous in that it could suggest wedding rings as well as social practices that lead nowhere, the nuances of such words as "impostures" and "spoils" reflect unquestionably negative views of marriage as a type of entrapment.[26]

Moore uses quotations most often to describe the male figure, and in reshaping the words of male writers, she undercuts both his character and his language. In identifying the man as Adam, for example, she includes a quotation from Philip Littell's review of George Santayana that appeared in *The New Republic* in 1923. The snippet of Littell's words in the poem is "something feline, / something colubrine" (CP 63). In different ways, the two adjectives, "feline" and "colubrine," reflect a certain denigration of male power. A description of a male figure as colubrine is obvious and sexual; feline, however, is typically used in reference to a female and thus serves to diminish Adam's masculinity.

The passage Moore quotes reads as follows: "We were puzzled and we were fascinated, as if by something feline, by something colubrine, at the core of his loneliness."[27] Here, Littell is trying to explain his reaction and that of his peers on reading Santayana's early verse in the *Harvard Monthly*. Littell says that no one could have known at that time that Santayana wanted to "remold his heart's desire" through his poetry. Although this review has only praise for Santayana's work, terms such as "feline" and "colubrine" indicate Littell's own discomfort with the poetry, a mixture of fear and distrust that causes him to distance himself with a feeling nearing distaste. Certainly, this fear and distaste are the sentiments that linger when the quotation is transplanted into the Eden of "Marriage."[28]

Adam's speech, too, is unnerving, but mostly because he pontificates on subjects about which he knows little and on which he has misguided opinions. In her description of Adam's blundering ramblings to Eve, Moore writes that he is "Treading chasms / on the uncertain footing of a spear" (CP 64). Moore's phrase is an adaptation of William Hazlitt's words in his essay on Edmund Burke's style "On the Prose-Style of Poets": "It may be said to pass yawning gulfs 'on the unstedfast footing of a spear.'"[29] Hazlitt is expressing his admiration of Burke's ability to maneuver through tricky sections of argument with the ease of a warrior. In its new position in Moore's poem, however, Hazlitt's language loses its laudatory aspects and becomes a sneering critique of one who would take the risk of trying to pretend that he knows things of which he is ignorant, "forgetting," as the poem says, "that there is in woman / a quality of mind / which as an instinctive manifestation is unsafe" (CP 64).

"Marriage" also includes a long quotation from Edward Thomas's *Feminine Influence on the Poets*, a work of literary criticism published in 1910.[30] Thomas describes at great length "The Kingis Quair," a poem written by King James I, in which the king depicts his love for Joan Beaufort, the daughter of the Earl of Somerset. Thomas writes of King James's first sight of Beaufort in the garden outside his prison:

> Her dress looped up carelessly to walk in that fresh morning of nightingales in the new-leaved thickets. . . . The nightingale stops singing. He dares not clap his hands to make it go on lest it should fly off; if he does nothing it will sleep; if he calls out it will not understand; and he begs the wind to shake the leaves and awake the song. And the bird sings again.[31]

In "Marriage," Moore quotes these words almost exactly: "He dares not clap his hands / to make it go on / lest it should fly off; / if he does nothing, it will sleep; / if he cries out, it will not understand" (CP 65). Prior to this, however, Moore had presented Adam as "plagued by the nightingale / in the new leaves / with its silence" (CP 64). Thus, whereas King James's poem is a gentle description of love at first sight, Moore twists the quotation to indicate frustration—the male is unable to get his bird to sing. Just by being married, the poem implies, the husband assumes that he can control the wife, the bird, and decide when and how she should give him pleasure. Instead, he looks merely foolish in his failure to manipulate her.

As unsettled as he is by woman and by his desire, sexual or otherwise (that "illusory fire"), Adam "stumbles over marriage," which, quoting William Godwin, Moore describes as "'a very trivial object indeed'" (CP 65). To Godwin, one recalls, marriage is a silly institution, a "method . . . for a thoughtless and romantic youth of each sex to come together, to see each other for a few times and under circumstances full of delusion, and then to vow eternal attachment."[32] Godwin believed that marriage should be abolished or at least rendered readily dissolvable. Moore's inclusion of his opinions of marriage in her description of that "First Marriage" thus undercuts any serious thoughts that Adam might have entertained about the institution.

Even love, that most revered of human emotions, is belittled through Moore's *déchirage* adaptation in this poem of a quotation from Anthony Trollope's *Barchester Towers*. Although Moore renders it, "for love that will / gaze an eagle blind, / that is with Hercules / climbing the trees / in the garden of the Hesperides, from forty-five to seventy / is the best age" (CP 66), Trollope's actual wording is:

> But for real, true love, love at first sight, love to devotion, love that robs a man of his sleep, love that will "gaze an eagle blind," love that "will hear the lowest sound when the suspicious tread of theft is stopped," love that is "like a Hercules, still climbing trees in the Hesperides,"—we believe the best age is from forty-five to seventy.[33]

This is a description of Mr. Thorne, a rural squire of the extinct type, who is infatuated with the manipulative yet paralyzed Signora Madeline Vesey Neroni. Trollope is being highly cynical of love here, but Moore's reshaping of his quotation does not indicate this. She has "cut out" Trollope's phrase, a phrase that is in fact a quotation drawn from elsewhere, in order to shape it to her own devices. Specifically, she connects the absurdity of overwhelming passion—"'love that will / gaze an eagle blind'"—with the idea that love and marriage are "a fine art," "an experiment, / a duty or . . . merely recreation." Moore overturns the male perspective of marriage as a serious and dignified commitment and presents it as a frivolous pastime.

The "irony" of the now-artificial state of the love relationship is "preserved" in literature and mythology, specifically in the banquet that Esther set up for Haman and Ahasuerus and in the silly, mismatched love of Caliban for Miranda in *The Tempest*. "Good monster, lead the way" (CP 67) is taken from *The Tempest* and changed from "O brave monster! lead the way," one of Stefano's lines.[34] This quotation's position in Shakespeare's play connects it with the buffoonery of Stefano and Trinculo; its position in "Marriage," however, relates it to the banquet that Esther engineered in order to save her people and is designed to suggest the nastiness of the marital relation. The "Ahasuerus *tête-à-tête* banquet" suggests that each spouse enters marriage with a separate agenda, which they will enforce using whatever sexual and emotional power they can bring to bear, as Esther does to persuade Ahasuerus to kill Haman and to save her people (CP 67).

During the most combative section of the poem, where the repartee of the man and the woman is at its height, the man decries the very existence of women when he says that "the fact of woman / is 'not the sound of the flute / but very poison'" (CP 67). This quotation is an adaptation of a passage from Abraham Mitram Rihbany's *The Syrian Christ* (1916), which is an explanation of customs described in the Bible. Moore embellished her note on this quotation by saying, "Silence of women—'to an Oriental, this is as poetry set to music,'" even though "not the sound of the flute but very poison" does not appear in *The Syrian Christ*.[35] Instead, Rihbany writes that it is important for women to remain silent in public, and he adds, "To oriental ears, as perhaps to Puritan ears of the good old type, such words are poetry set to music," but he never refers to a flute or to poison.[36] In this case, Moore relegated Rihbany's words to her notes and used them as mere inspiration for the man's opening salvo in his argument with the woman, a volley that stings in its misogyny.

In "Marriage," the explicit argument between the male and female voices (as explored by Lynn Keller and Cristanne Miller) solidifies the "dialectical interaction between the work and the world" that Stephen Bann has identified as a feature of collage.[37] The quotations create a reverberation in the poem between the intent and the context, between the original words and the new meaning they acquire by being placed in radically different surroundings. In this way Moore is able to "subvert" tradition, both formally and institutionally. Within the poem, in other words, Moore is not constrained by external influence, conventional or otherwise. In fact, her use of this technique constitutes an adaptation of the Socratic method of refuting all sides of the argument. Dialogue allows Moore to remove herself from the context of the poem so that the critique of marriage implicit in the poem does not reflect on the poet.

During the course of this dialogue between the male and the female—really it is open warfare—the woman's attitude toward men as insignificant and unstable is registered through a quotation: "This butterfly, / this waterfly, this nomad / that has 'proposed / to settle on my hand for life'— / What can one do with it?" (CP 68). This quotation is from Charles Reade's novel *Christie Johnstone* (1853). In this silly romance, a young, aristocratic gentleman, Lord Ipsden, who has "neither vices nor virtues," who is wealthy but does absolutely nothing, asks his cousin once removed, Lady Barbara Sinclair, for her hand in marriage. Lady Barbara refuses him because she has "kept herself in reserve for some earnest man, who was not to come flattering and fooling to her, but look another way and do exploits." On considering Lord Ipsden's proposal, Lady Barbara thinks: "Accustomed to measure men by their character alone and to treat with sublime contempt the accidents of birth and fortune, she had been a little staggered by the assurance of this butterfly that had proposed to settle on her hand—for life."[38] Treating men as butterflies is a reversal of male and female roles and is a dismissal of the effectiveness of men. Lord Ipsden, and men in general, are superficial, useless, insignificant, and narcissistic.

Adam's final word in this dialogue is that there are many people other than artists who are "fools" because they get married. Adam, however, as the next line reminds us, has forgotten that "some have merely rights while some have obligations" (CP 68). The allusion here is to the words of Edmund Burke, who had written: "Asiatics have rights; Europeans have obligations."[39] The obligations of Burke's "Europeans" are like those of men in marriage: behavior structured around the inherent condition of male condescension toward women, the European superior attitude toward its colonies and the male assumption of higher authority over the wife. The British cultural imperialism is analogous here to male hegemony.[40]

Men and women, however, are too self-involved to be fit to participate in relations with each other. Though the woman may profess to her husband that she is at his "command," she belies her avowal by leaving him for no more reason than that she has "seen enough of him," and so does not really show "petrine fidelity," though the alternate image of her rocklike composure filters through (CP 69). This quotation of Simone Puget's advertisement in the *English Review* of June 1914 is highly cynical, referring to wives as "pretty dolls" and to their husbands as "peaceful." Moore's inclusion of Puget's words emphasizes her opinion that marriage is an outdated social form, despite its appeal.

At the conclusion of the poem, Moore quotes Daniel Webster's phrase, "Liberty and union / now and forever," in order to show that the control of a social institution such as marriage is similar to the immutable, implacable form of the motto—neither is ideally suited to anyone. Respected public figures reinforce this idea by treating marriage reductively, as if the complexity of the relationship could be regarded as a matter of ritual, of established "simplicity" (CP 69). The quotation from Webster is optimistic but misguided as applied to marriage, just as Moore sees those who view life as a matter of habits—"the Book on the writing-table; / the hand in the breast-pocket"—as underestimating the overwhelming variety of human nature and relations (CP 70). Moore believes that "Liberty and union" is oxymoronic when applied to marriage, and the statue of Webster in the park is emblematic of the pompously blind nature of man who lives by habits rather than by understandings. According to Margaret Holley, a motto constitutes "a special form of quotation, of language fixed and produced, just as the emblem is a special form of spatial imagery, culturally fixed and reproduced."[41] Moore does not change the motto from the statue because she cannot—it is "fixed." Her use of this quotation suggests Moore's feeling that our culture is unwilling or unable to change, particularly with respect to such immutable institutions as marriage.

Moore's use of a collage technique thus becomes her way of questioning marriage in an oblique fashion. She apparently felt that her early drafts of the poem were too angry, or perhaps too personal, to produce a sustained critique. By resorting to collage, with its rejection of traditional, mimetic art forms, Moore was able to register her criticisms of the social institution without risking direct confrontation with cultural standards. By allying herself with artists who turned their backs on traditions of perspective in the visual arts, Moore also subverts traditions of perspective in the cultural sphere: a rejection of marriage is a rejection of traditional views of reality. In addition, the collage juxtaposition of unrelated pieces of history and social commentary is also Moore's way of dramatizing the nature of the marital relationship itself—two unrelated people with little or nothing in common (as Moore would have it) thrown into a union "without any connectives to express the quality of their relationship."

In creating works of collage, the artist is like the anthropologist who makes "the familiar strange," in James Clifford's words, so that we can reassess the art and artifacts of our own culture as if it were not our own.[42] Moore makes an effort at this: not only does she make the familiar words of the past "strange" by editing them and placing them in a new context, she makes marriage "strange" and provides a reassessment of an institution that is generally taken for granted. In doing so, Moore gives a practical—what one might refer to as a female—focus to the collagist's attempt to "marry" art forms. Not only does she employ collage techniques, she encourages us to see how they are applicable to "real" situations. In this way collage also allows her to change the possibilities of that "reality."

"An Octopus" takes the international approach of the collage form of "Marriage" and applies it directly to America.[43] If "Marriage" is an antimanifesto, then "An Octopus" is Moore's effort at a manifesto—a directive of appropriate (i.e., fulfilling, unrepressive, imaginative, and unmaterialistic) behavior.[44] Instead of drawing quotations from a seemingly random series of sources, as in "Marriage," Moore restricted herself to sources directly connected with her subject. She composed the first half of the poem from two guidebooks, one of America and one of the Canadian Rockies. Moore's other primary source was the Department of the Interior's guide to Mt. Rainier.

While previous critics have discussed the relevance of Greek philosophy to Moore's Christian ethics of love, or described Mt. Rainier as merely an "octopus of ice" in this poem, I would like to extend this reading to the poet.[45] She, the poet herself, is the octopus, her long tentacles gathering information from a wide variety of sources and drawing together unrelated facts to build the poem. The octopus is of ice because it tries to avoid emotional entanglement in its techniques of observation and collection. The resulting catalogue of plants, animals, colors, and minerals represents the surface description used to explain human existence, as the Greeks did.[46] They, as the poem says, "liked smoothness, distrusting what was back / of what could not be clearly seen" (O 88). Sheer description of the physical appearance of naturally occurring phenomena will, according to the ancient Greek philosophers, present the parameters of our existence; to Moore, as to the painters, the colors and textures of the external world continue to impinge upon us no matter how fervently we retreat from them through abstraction.

Nonetheless, as with "Marriage," Moore continues in this poem to insert quotations out of their original contexts, but most of the quotations in "An Octopus" come from *Rules and Regulations, Mount Rainier National Park, Washington, 1922,* of the Department of the Interior

Rules and Regulations. This is a pamphlet that Moore picked up on one of her trips with her mother to visit her brother, who was stationed in the navy in Seattle. On the first of the two trips that Moore took west, she climbed Mt. Rainier. "An Octopus" is the direct result of this experience.[47] In fact, the poem is organized very similarly to the pamphlet, with separate sections on animal life, mineral deposits, and geographical description.

However, as with "Marriage," Moore plays around with the idea of quotation.[48] Usually, words are bracketed by quotation marks when they have been transplanted in exact form from the work of another. Moore still almost always changes the wording of a quotation when she transposes it into her poetry, as perhaps her tease of the literary establishment. In "An Octopus," in fact, she changes some quotations so radically that they are hard to trace to their original source. In other places, Moore actually uses exact quotations but does not mark them with quotation marks.

I believe that Moore has a similar purpose behind her collage technique in this poem as in "Marriage:" she wants to reinforce an ideal of culture while at the same time wanting to denigrate it. In the case of "An Octopus," Moore wants to re-create the American sublime of the transcendentalists and the Hudson School through a clear evocation of the grandeur of American natural splendor, but at the same time she wants to harpoon the romantic ideal of the sublime through her insertion of her family's pet names for each other and through her ostensibly serious regard for the Department of the Interior's rules and regulations, as well as through her continued "adjustment" of quotations.[49]

The Rosenbach Museum and Library has a xerox of the original pamphlet from the Department of the Interior, the original having been lost or misplaced. Even so, Moore's notations are clear. She read the pamphlet carefully, underlined passages that interested her, and edited various phrases that she was considering for the long poem. For example, the pamphlet reads at one point: "The steep upper slopes of the spurs diverging from the main ridges are frequently covered with a stunted, scraggy growth of *low trees firmly rooted in the crevices between the rocks . . . [B]ent and twisted by the wind, . . . the trunks are quite prostrate, and the crowns are flattened mats of branches* lying close to the ground" (Moore's emphasis).[50] Moore combines this quotation with one from Clifton Johnson's *What to See in America*, a sightseeing guide:

"They [snow crystals] cut the bark [from the] trees . . . shear off the tender twigs that have started [to grow out during the summer,] the winds bending the tree so that it has the appearance of trying to escape flying sand, cold, and nine months of snow. They seldom grow higher than eight feet and many grow along the ground like vines."[51] In the final version of "An Octopus" these quotations become: "Is tree the word for these strange things / 'flat on the ground like vines'; / some 'bent in a half circle with branches on one side / suggesting dustbrushes, not trees; / some finding strength in union, forming little stunted groves / their flattened mats of branches shrunk in trying to escape.'" (O 89). Here we can see that Moore transmutes "along the ground like vines" into "flat on the ground like vines" and that she has united in one quotation the park portfolio's "flattened mats of branches" with Johnson's idea of "escape."

Moore neglected to use quotation marks completely for several other pieces taken from both Johnson and Wilcox. "The Goat's Mirror" comes from Wilcox's description of Lake Agnes, "Goats' Looking Glass," while "in the shape of the left human / foot" is Wilcox's way to describe Lake Louise.[52] Although Moore uses quotation marks to acknowledge Johnson's portrayal of the petrified forests of America's southwest, she mixes one section, where he refers to the "Blue Forest," with another, where he says that "there are certain slopes where [the trees lie] tumbled together as if whole quarries of marble and onyx had been dynamited," to create in the poem "'blue forests thrown together with marble and jasper and agate / as if whole quarries had been dynamited" (O 84–85). Two lines previous to this, however, she uses no quotation marks to show her debt to Johnson when she writes, "Composed of calcium gems and alabaster pillars," which comes directly from Johnson's "pendant with calcium gems, pillared in alabaster" (O 84).[53]

The question arises of Moore's motivation with regard to these types of quotation rearrangements. Why would such a meticulous reader and notetaker conflate and rewrite quotations when she then goes so far as to cite sources for them in her "Notes" section of the *Complete Poems*? In the fabulous notebook at the Rosenbach Museum and Library that contains the entire poetic process of "Marriage" and "An Octopus," as well as other poems, Moore gives page references for each quotation. Why would someone who is this careful then refuse to transplant quotations verbatim? Clearly, her methods of revision are at work here; her insistence on the right word takes precedence over scholastic faithfulness. In fact, through this notebook, it is possible to trace Moore's poetic process. The original quotations change on the way to the notebook and change again on the way into the poem.

However, I believe that Moore was toying with us in addition to her poetic sensibilities. She ostensibly is quoting Johnson exactly when she writes, "'thoughtful beavers / making drains which seem the work of careful men with / shovels'" (O 84). Her note for this line in *Complete Poems* says, "bristling, puny, swearing men" (CP 273). The quotation from her notebook from Johnson says, "puny, bristling, swearing men with saws."[54] In this case Moore has sanitized the grim reality of the rough men in the wilderness to make them "careful." She also has inserted the beaver, which is not native to the Mt. Rainier area but which was her family's nickname for Mary Norcross, a family friend. By denuding this scene of the sweat and bad language of men, Moore retreats from the dirtiness of actuality to the fairyland of books such as *Wind in the Willows,* whose characters' names became nicknames for the Moore family members.[55]

This insertion of family names often appears in Moore's poetry. As Willis indicates, an earlier version of "An Octopus" uses Moore's brother's nickname, badger, in place of the real animal to be found in this region, the marmot. In fact, the parks pamphlet describes the marmot as "about the size of a badger," which must have triggered a response in Moore.[56] Even Wilcox refers to the connections between the two animals when he mentions "the great hoary marmot, or whistling badger."[57] While Moore changed the badger into a marmot for her later *Complete Poems* version, the *Observations* version of this poem keeps the badger in the poem, as out of context as it might be: "'when you hear the best wild music of the forest / it is sure to be a badger,' / the victim on some slight observatory, / of 'a struggle between curiosity and caution' / inquiring what has scared it" (O 86). Moore drew these quotations from several separate sentences. Under the subtitle "Hoary Marmot," the parks brochure states:

> Any animal of heavy-bodied appearance about the size of a badger, noted on the rock slides or in the green meadows near by, *is sure to be a marmot.* . . . The clear and penetrating *whistle of the* hoary *marmot* is *among the best of the wild music of the mountain.* . . . The reposeful demeanor of the marmot as it sits quietly on some convenient rock as one approaches, gives little evidence of the struggle between curiosity and caution taking place within.[58] (Moore's emphasis)

The play of Moore's collage technique is most apparent in her quotations from the parks manual. The list of regulations in this brochure is long and somewhat absurd, and her inclusion of them in the poem indicates one of the effects of collage on perspective. By treating everything in the poem as if it had equal importance, single-point perspective is destroyed. These quotations include "names and addresses of persons to notify / in case of disaster" (O 86) and "guns, nets, seines, traps and explosives, / hired vehicles, gambling and intoxicants are prohibited, / disobedient persons being summarily removed / and not allowed to return without permission in writing" (O 89). The poem addresses the silliness of these rules two lines earlier: "these odd oracles of cool official sarcasm."

As part of her "homework" for this poem, Moore read two magazine articles on the behavior and appearance of the octopus. The parks manual itself refers to Mt. Rainier as "A Glacial Octopus" in the subtitle to a photograph on it, so it is clear that Moore did not make the connection between the mountain and the animal on her own.[59] However, it is characteristic of her that she would investigate the octopus so that she could refer to it factually in the poem. Here again, though, Moore distorts the quotations when she places them in the poem. Where the poem says, "'ghostly pallor changing / to the green metallic tinge of an anemone-starred pool'" (O 83), the article by Frances Ward in the *Illustrated London News* says, "If frightened, an intense ghostly pallor passes right over the animal, and it tries to escape by suddenly swimming away; . . . The delicate green metallic tinge is due to iridocysts below the layer of colour cells."[60] "Anemone-starred pool," however lovely a phrase, appears nowhere in this article on the octopus; it is a complete fabrication of Moore's, yet remains within quotation marks, removing her responsibility for it.

This poem does not pretend to have a goal; its circular motion imitates that of the lost wanderer: "Completing a circle, / you have been deceived into thinking that you have progressed" (O 83–84). And the poem itself has a circular movement, beginning with the "octopus / / of ice" and ending with the "relentless accuracy . . . of this octopus" (O 89) and the "glassy octopus symmetrically pointed" (O 90). The poem moves outward in all directions, just as the tentacles of the octopus stretch out in the shape of a circle.[61] The fragments of naturalist information move in concentric circles outward, as if the poet were standing in the middle of the forest and turning slowly in all directions to take in, portion by portion, all that the American flora and fauna can present.[62]

This octopus is "deceptively reserved," meaning that the poem is not as coldly observational as it would appear, leading us in the direction of Henry James's surface coolness disrupted by his underlying passion. Near the end of the poem are the lines: "damned for its sacrosanct remoteness— / like Henry James 'damned by the public for decorum'; / not decorum but restraint; / it was the love of doing hard things / that rebuffed and wore them out—a public out of sympathy / with neatness" (O 89). Here the poet expresses her fear that, although her technique of removed observation is embraced by such masters as Henry James, it is out of favor with her audience. Close observation is the most difficult of skills, but it looks too detached to be popular. The octopus and the poet, then, seem to be coolly unemotional, but they are really just trying to give order to a myriad of artifacts—in this case, those of the American wilderness.

Collage works for Moore as a tool for political transgressiveness, a method that is especially apt for her because of its distance from her personally. Because she draws quotations from sources apart from herself, the sources, rather than the poet herself, bear responsibility for the content of the words. Even though she reworks the quotations, often for a more biting result than given by their original sources, they remain tied to their first context, so that Moore's caustic remarks seem not to derive from her but from her sources. The technique of collage, then, enables her to denigrate entrenched social institutions, such as marriage and the established use of elite sources for literature, by using quotations from the Parks Service Manual for "An Octopus." This social critique appears not just in Moore's collage, however, but in her adaptation of photomontage, which the next chapter will demonstrate.

4
Dada Subversion: Hannah Höch and Marianne Moore

I am not going to attempt to claim that Marianne Moore was a radical dadaist in disguise.[1] I am, however, going to propose that she had many of the same goals and used many of the same techniques as the dada artist Hannah Höch did in her photomontages. In their artistic productions, both of these artists felt compelled to conceal the primary purpose of their work through the subterfuge of their photomontage techniques, techniques that force careful research in order to unpeel the disguising layers of obfuscation. Both of these artists are also highly moral in tone, by which I mean that they each have a specific lesson in mind when they compose their work; they desire to influence their audience's behavior and opinions.[2] In doing so, both Moore and Höch reject modernist tendencies to place art in a sphere external to society by reinserting artistic productions directly into their own cultures, with the dual, yet conflicting, function of criticism of those cultures, but also of solutions and of re-creations. In addition, lest these artists seem not to be allied with the dada movement, each of them relies on a method of composition based on chance and chaos rather than on logic, a technique that takes the form in Moore's work, for instance, of tangential remarks and illogical sequence of subjects and statements.

Moore was not compelled to translate only photomontage into the poetic sphere, however. Her adaptation of Man Ray's rayograph technique, whereby the translucence of the images destroys foreground-to-background movement, appears in such a poem as "Radical," about a carrot, which was apparently too directly subversive for her to permit its inclusion in the later collection, *The Complete Poems*. By drawing the foreground and background into direct adherence, rather than placing them in their traditionally hierarchical relationship, Man Ray and Moore undermine bourgeois standards of relative importance.

Most importantly, however, Moore works into poetry the technique of photomontage. Her collage method, as I discussed in the previous chapter, works by pulling quotations from varied sources and reshaping them before placing them in the new context of her poems. Her photomontage technique is similar, but instead of operating on the level of quotations, she transplants images, also from various sources, and also reshapes them before "pasting" them into her poems.[3] As with photomontage, there are rarely any connectives between these images—they take on the chaotic nature of random juxtaposition.

The moment of inception of the dada movement has been well-documented, although, like the course of the movement itself, even the beginning of the movement is filled with contradiction.[4] What is essential is that the word "dada" was chosen as a sound, a sound to which no meaning could be attached. As the focal point of the movement, the title comes to represent the nothingness that the dadaists embraced. By turning to this nothingness, the dadaists expressed the betrayal they felt at the development of the First World War. The catastrophe and devastation that Europe faced at this time were unparalleled, and the dadaists believed that it was the bourgeoisie, with its emphasis on the rational means-end view of life, that had led the Continent into war.

The dada movement was a truly international phenomenon; it surfaced more or less concurrently in Switzerland, America, France, Russia, and Germany. The German dada moment was short, as all dada occurrences were, lasting only from 1918 to 1923.[5] Unlike the Swiss movement, which reacted against the horror of the war, the German one focused primarily on the postwar political chaos, particularly on the corruption and impotence of the Weimar Republic government, the one that enabled Adolf Hitler to achieve sole control of the country quickly.[6] The Berlin dadaists, among them Richard Huelsenbeck, Wieland Herzfeld, John Heartfield, Raoul Hausmann, Hannah Höch, and Max Ernst, were left-wing communists devoted to political propaganda. Höch and Hausmann originated the photomontage technique as a venue for political activism because the Weimar censors were severe and photomontage concealed the overt message of the artist.[7]

Because its primary focus was to shake up the bourgeoisie, much of the dada productions were ephemeral in nature: manifestations, bruitism, and simultaneous readings of random selection, such as the daily newspaper. The dadaists felt, probably correctly, that they had to reject traditional forms of art that society had accepted—traditional perspective in painting, naturalistic forms in figurative sculpture, sequential narrative in fiction, and established conventions in lyrical poetry—in order to express most clearly their disgust with the rationalism that these art forms represented. Hugo Ball's Cabaret Voltaire, for instance, presented evenings of bizarrely dressed people who danced randomly and made unmusical sounds.[8]

By dismissing traditional art, an art that fit into Adorno's theory of "autonomous" art, as I discussed in a previous chapter, the dadaists reinserted art into culture. Their art is radically rebellious, but because it has such a deeply felt moral intention, it is not merely critical of its engendering culture but also a creative force in the attempt to reshape that culture.[9] Raoul Hausmann emphasized the political force of the photomontage when he described it as having "an inherent propagandistic power that contemporary life was not courageous enough to absorb and to develop."[10]

Dada, in fact, was not only the attempt to discredit the war, it was the effort to take advantage of the dis-ease that the war had yielded in order to rejuvenate art's place in society as a way to undermine the bourgeoisie and to reinvigorate irrationality as an appropriate approach to life.[11] Tristan Tzara in 1922 explained the dada urge to reenter society:

> Art is not the most precious manifestation of life. Art has not the celestial and universal power that people like to attribute to it. Life is far more interesting. Dada knows the correct measure that should be given to art: with subtle, perfidious methods, Dada introduces it into daily life. And vice versa.[12]

In a seemingly paradoxical manner, and in spite of their fury with the excessive rationality of the bourgeoisie, the dadaists viewed technology with not mere acceptance but avid endorsement.[13] This eagerness is readily apparent on a perusal of their photocollages. Machines and machine parts recur constantly, often taking the place of essential parts of the human anatomy, such as the head. Oddly enough, the dadaists connected their passion for machinery to their adherence to chaos and chance. They turned to chance as a method of composition because it is antithetical to rational or logical decision making and because it requires the same lack of intention that a machine has in its productions.

Chance decisions, the dadaists felt, are equivalent to the decisions made by a machine because they are equally mechanically derived. One of the ways the dadaists arrived at this notion was through their belief that humans have no soul. "Why have spirit," Hausmann asks in *Der Dada 3*, "in a world which runs on mechanically?" In fact, as Hannah Höch explained in an interview, the dadaists intended their photocollages to look like they were "entirely composed by a machine."[14] Technology, as represented in the photomontages, then, is a positive image of hope and salvation for the dadaists, rather than an image of impending doom.

A prime example of photomontage, and one that sets up what Marianne Moore is doing in her poetry, is Hannah Höch's "Schnitt mit dem Küchenmesser Dada durch die letzte weimarer Bierbauchkulturepoche Deutschlands" (Cut with the Kitchen Knife Dada through the Last Weimar Beer Belly Cultural Epoch of Germany), 1919–20. I will not go into much detail about Höch's collage, as Gertrud Jula Dech and Maud Lavin have already covered this territory.[15] What I would like to stress, instead, is Höch's moral lesson, her concealment of her overt meaning, her chaotic composition and her enthusiasm for technology.[16]

Dech has done extensive research on this collage in order to explain it fully. She identifies the original source of nearly every photograph in the photomontage, making identification of the figures in the photographs possible. Without Dech's work, however, the photomontage falls flat. It expresses the chaotic nature of the dada manifesto, but it has little artistic merit. The tonal qualities of the images have merged over time, so there is little dynamic movement through lights and darks—only a muddy sea of faces and gears.[17] Ignorance of the identity of these faces is the final blow to an appreciation of this piece, however. The work cannot carry the weight of art solely on the weakened merits of its composition; it requires its original content to rejuvenate it as a work of art, such as the reinvigorating efforts of Dech's research.

The problems of composition and content evidenced by this work are problems that turn into merits in Moore's work but that derive from similar sources. Both artists felt compelled to obscure the original meanings of their work: Höch for fear of political censorship and worse, Moore for fear of disturbing the implacable nature of the American bourgeoisie. Each of them works from the basis of a seemingly illogical

Hannah Höch (1889–1978). *Schnitt mit dem Küchenmesser Dada durch die letzte weimarer Bierbauchkulturepoche Deutschlands* (Cut with the Kitchen Knife Dada through the Last Weimar Beer Belly Cultural Epoch of Germany), 1919–20. Photomontage, 114 X 90 cm. Nationalgalerie Staatliche Museen Preussischer Kulturbesitz Berlin. © ARS.

underlying structure: Höch with the dancing patterns of people flying sporadically across her field, Moore with the erratic leaping from one subject to another and with the conflation of several subjects into one.[18]

Both of these artists are strongly invested in problems with their culture and society. In the antidadaist section appearing in its upper right, Höch's collage shows Wilhelm II, the emperor of Germany who had to abdicate his throne in 1918. By replacing this unpopular leader's mustaches with photographs of wrestlers to emphasize his absurdity, and by encircling him with equally unpopular military leaders, Höch indicates her displeasure with the dreadful state he created in the country. She reinforces this critique by placing a photograph of hoards of unemployed people in a Berlin street next to his left cheek. Höch could get away with this type of political dissension only through a technique such as photomontage. Its elusive form deflects overt readings of its political content.

Höch's photomontage is interlaced with technological images, primarily circular in shape. A gear divides the science section from the Weimar section; a ball-bearing wheel next to a girder stacks on a series of representations of technology, including a car, in order to separate the science section from the "mass of humanity" quadrant. A wheel spilling its ball bearings lifts the central dancer in the air. In dada iconography, technology-as-the-human-mind represents the ability of the innovations of science to lead men to make appropriate decisions. This image appears on three important occasions here: Einstein, Marx, and Hausmann all have machines growing out of their heads. As I said earlier, the dadaists viewed technology as an answer to the disillusion of the early twentieth century, a belief that plays itself out in Höch's collage.

Dada had a strong presence in America. In fact, it probably started earlier there than in Zurich, though the American movement did not adopt the dada title until later.[19] Marcel Duchamp and Francis Picabia both came to New York in 1915 and joined up with the art circle already in formation there consisting of Alfred Stieglitz, Man Ray, Walter Arensberg, Katharine Drier, and others. It was when he was in New York, for instance, that Duchamp put the *Fountain* up in the Independent Artists exhibition in 1917, the urinal that was exhibited behind a curtain and then withdrawn.[20]

Because America was not yet involved in the First World War in 1915, and because the effects of the war on America were not nearly as devastating as on Europe, dada had a different character in New York than in Berlin. It still had its wild happenings and its manifestos and its radical publications, but it was not nearly as politically charged. Estera Milman explains this difference by saying that "just as Paris Dada reacted to the cultural implications of postwar France, New York Dada . . . responded to the social realities of America and thus retained its modernist inclinations."[21] One implication of this remark is that dada in America was not engaged in the bursting desire of the European dada movement to reinvest art into the culture but was in fact content with art's external role in a perhaps more strongly bourgeois culture than that existing in Europe; another implication of Milman's statement is that American dada had no investment in political engagement.

I disagree with this assessment of the New York dada movement because of its expression through such art forms as the readymades of Duchamp and the montages of Moore. Much criticism has been written on the relation of Duchamp's work to appropriation and on appropriation's direct connections to a critique of the commodification of bourgeois life.[22] Moore's work is also socially and politically involved, but like the German photomontagists, she obscures her political content through her technique, an elusiveness that has allowed her political activism to be largely ignored.

The issue becomes here, why in a society that was not nearly as repressive as Weimar Germany did Moore feel compelled to veil her censure of it? I can only speculate that her reasons were related to the conventionality of American society, a conventionality so extreme that it could little tolerate social or political condemnation, particularly that coming from a woman. In *New York, 1913: The Armory Show and the Paterson Strike Pageant,* Martin Green explains the tensions between popular culture and elite culture that might also explain Moore's sensitivity toward social recrimination deriving from reception of her poetry. Green argues that the Puritan ethic promoted materialism and work over spiritual values, and that the artists of the early twentieth century, in trying to reject this standard, "made [their] art difficult and esoteric." "Art values," as Green terms them, were radically separated from "social values," forcing the artist to become a revolutionary, to the extent of becoming "anti-Christian," an ultimate transgression for Moore.[23] Green continues by saying, "This was a guerilla war against the bourgeois class and its hegemony."[24]

Kristeva reinforces an understanding of the conflicted situation in which Moore found herself by describing the role of art in culture in general as transgressive:

> Poetry emerged alongside sacrifice as the expenditure of the thesis establishing the sociosymbolic order and as the bringing into play of the vehemence of drives through the positing of language. . . . The problem, then, was one of finding practices of expenditure capable of confronting the machine, colonial expansion, banks, science, Parliament—those positions of mastery that conceal their violence and pretend to be more neutral legality. Recovering the subject's vehemence required a descent into the structural positing of social order; it required a descent into the structural positing of the thetic in language so that violence, surging up through the phonetic, syntactic, and logical orders, could reach the symbolic order and the technocratic ideologies that had been built over this violence to ignore or repress it. To penetrate the era, poetry had to disturb the logic that dominated the social order and do so through that logic itself, by assuming and unraveling its position, its synthesis, and hence the ideologies it controls.[25]

I quote such a long passage from Kristeva because it so clearly illuminates the issues that Moore faced. Only by taking on, in the sense of investing in, the prevailing culture can one transgress it, so Moore was always forced to be truly ambivalent in her attitudes and in her poetry. She had to embrace tradition in order to critique it. This ambivalence is apparent in such situations as dadaism's marvel at the machine and technology. America worshipped the machine, and as I will argue later in my discussions of "Camellia Sabina" and "The Jerboa," Moore took on the language of science and technology, thereby appropriating and adopting it but only in order to subvert it.

Leavell identifies American interest in machinery with a quotation that expresses the extent of enthusiasm with technology but that also reiterates the Puritan devotion to materialism and the strength of the Puritan heritage in America: "America—made of the Puritan, by the Puritan, for the Puritan, remade of the Machine, by the Machine, for the Machine."[26] The rest of this quotation indicates America's final interest in the cultural and spiritual spheres of artistic endeavor, but as Green has argued, the turn toward the elitism of "high" art was in direct opposition to the hegemony of the bourgeoisie in America.

Moore has a series of poems in her *Selected Poems* that illustrates her devotion to scientific method and to the type of logic that the dadaists embraced in their turn to technology, including "Camellia Sabina," "The Jerboa," and "Radical."[27] Also like the dadaists, though, Moore undercuts this interest in rationality through her poetic devices of disjunction and improbable juxtaposition of images in her adaptation of photomontage to modern poetry.

"Camellia Sabina" expresses this ambivalence toward logical progression through its form of a list of flowers, each type of which generates a spreading fan of tangential description and association so that in her concentration on the flowers themselves, Moore takes on the role of the rational scientist, and through the spinning reflections that the flowers produce, she takes on the more chaotic characteristics of the dada poet.[28] Thus her reflection on the illustration on the label of a jar of plums evolves into a discussion of grapes through an inversion of scale along the lines of *Gulliver's Travels.*

The narrator is examining a bottle of plums from France. The label tells her where the plums are from, "Marmande (France) in parenthesis," and who has packaged them, "Alexis Godillot." The bottle itself is green and handblown, with the initials of the bottler, "A. G.," blown "unevenly" into the glass next to an air bubble (CP 16). "They are a fine duet" refers back to the title and the first line, the flower and the plum on the label, but then the poem reverts to lyrical description in the incantatorial style of Gerard Manley Hopkins: "graft-grown briar-black bloom / on black-thorn pigeon's blood" (CP 16). Tying this extravagantly baroque interlude into the poem is the narrator's calmly scientific voice, describing the "screw-top" of the plum jar, "sealed with foil," and ending the stanza with the prim statement: "Appropriate custom."

Except for its brief moment of elaboration, this first stanza adheres to Moore's detached efforts to be the scientist. Even here, however, she cannot resist escape from rationalism. She feels compelled to leave pure description for the impassioned moment of alliteration, toying with the vowels driven by "grown," "bloom," "thorn," and "blood," and dissolving the guttural consonants of the *g*'s into the softer, more dissipated *b*'s. In addition, her final statement for the stanza has the high moral tone of the dada manifesto, with its fastidious intent. Yet, her tone is sarcastic, making her appear critical of the use of foil for the bottle lid, making her appear critical of the French and their customs.[29]

The second stanza moves into a closer, more scientific view of camellias. “And they keep under / glass also, camellias” pulls the first two stanzas together through the conjunction and the relation of the camellias to the plums, though the plums “keep” encased in glass while the camellias grow well in greenhouses. Here Moore takes on the role of the botanist, using words like “catalogued” and describing the flower in terms of the shape, color, and size of its petals: “Gloria mundi / with a leaf two inches, nine lines / broad” (CP 16).

As with the first stanza, though, Moore must undermine this detached and unemotional tone by disrupting the syntax of the sentences. This stanza begins with a pronoun, which would normally refer to the plums and camellias of the first stanza but which can only be meant to refer solely to the flowers. This inversion causes a reverberation between the stanzas, one that the poem resolves quickly but whose trace remains. Moore also inverts the lines describing the Gloria mundi variety of the flower by throwing the verb to the end of the sentence, forcing a suspension within the lines. She reinforces this suspension in the next lines by putting the verb at the end of a longer phrase, one which only finds resolution in the next stanza.

In this second stanza, too, Moore leaves her quietly remote voice of description for one of wit: “The French are a cruel race—willing / to squeeze the diner’s cucumber or broil a / meal on vine-shoots” (CP 16). Implicit in this remark, aside from the poet’s expressed amusement, is a critical tone directed at a people who would bottle plums in such a fashion or take such care with flowers or grapes. The poem cannot conceal the double layer of humor, with its overt denial of seriousness and underlying stratum of moral dismissiveness.

The sentence that bridges the second and third stanzas continues the scientific approach by comparing the camellia to the mushroom, the highly poisonous amanita. The camellia is as white as this mushroom and has the “pinwheel” shape of it. The only moment of overt poetic inspiration in this stanza comes next, with another connection to mushrooms: “pale / stripe that looks as if on a mushroom the / sliver from a beet-root carved into a rose were laid” (CP 16). Again, the verb comes at the end of the sentence, a sentence that is complex enough to require a pause for tracking the meaning. Only at the end of this sentence does the poet pull it down away from the elliptical; the state of hesitation lasts long enough to dismiss logic, to reject the status quo.

The rest of the third stanza is primarily a quotation from a book on gardening by the Abbé Berlèse, *The Monographie du Genre Camellia*, as Moore's note attests (CP 263):

> "Dry / the windows with a cloth fastened to a staff.
> In the camellia-house there must be
> no smoke from the stove, or dew on
>   the windows, lest the plants ail"
> the amateur is told;
>   "mistakes are irreparable and nothing will avail."
>
> (CP 16)

This section appears to be a clear scientific discussion of how to care for camellias, but Moore included it because it deviates from that intention in its particulars. The Abbé's direction for how to clean the windows, for instance, is amusing in its detail. Why do we need to know exactly how to clean the windows? Why with a staff? His threatening tone, too, stretches the rational veneer of his language. By saying, "nothing will avail," it is as if he is discussing the mortal illness of a human being rather than the care of something as insignificant as a flower. The satire produced by Moore's inclusion of this overinflation of concern proves her ultimate conflict between the objectivity of science and the allure of the imagination, with the escape from rationalism that it represents.

While the tone of the fourth stanza returns to the objective, its subject veers wildly away from the camellia, never to return until the last few lines of the poem. The tone is, therefore, only objective on the surface. Moore pretends an alliance to scientific methods of lists and descriptions, yet her form and content reject them, just as the dadaists rejected the form and content of lyrical poetry. The fourth stanza begins with the flower: "A scentless nosegay / is thus formed in the midst of the bouquet / from bottles, casks and corks" (CP 16–17). Moore's purpose, however, is unclear; she may be describing the illustrations of flowers on many bottles that "form" altogether a "bouquet"; she may, however, be bringing in the language of the wine taster—when a wine has a bouquet, it has a smell. Yet, this bouquet is "scentless." This confusion is intentional. Logic desires a clear reading of the poem; Moore disrupts logic to depict the true inaccuracy of rationality.

The rest of this stanza discusses wine and how important the Bordeaux imprint is to the wine business. Moore dismisses wine quickly, though, to turn to the grape itself, the grape meant for ingestion: "A / food-grape, however—'born / of nature and of art'—is true ground for the grape-holiday" (CP 17). The very meter of this line sets the mood for the excitement that the poet would like to engender at the thought of special grapes for eating. The spondee of "true ground" stops the poem, and the long vowels emphasize this cessation. The following two anapests speed the final words; the stressed long *a*'s lighten the tone even more.

Even so, the camellia has disappeared as a subject in this poem, and Moore turns here, at the fifth stanza, to small animals, a return to the ostensibly objective tone of the scientist but one that is, again, undermined by its lack of connection to the poem's originary topic. Moore wants to talk about the grape, however, and how the grape affects the life of the mice in Bordeaux. She first describes what normal mice might eat: "wild parsnip- or sunflower- or / morning-glory-seed, with an occasional / grape" (CP 17). Then, she imagines which mice might be able to eat grapes. Certainly, the "vines of the Bolzano / grape of Italy" might support mice.

Through the fifth stanza Moore shrinks the perspective of her audience from human scale down to that of the mouse. The poem starts with human-sized perception, with the appearance of a bottle of plums, but it must now reduce its view to the mouse's perspective. In this way, the next stanza can reproduce what the mouse sees and how the mouse considers its food. The poet emphasizes this treatment by speaking directly to the mouse here, as if the audience were the mouse: "In that well-piled / larder above your / head, the picture of what you will eat is looked at from the end of the avenue" (CP 17). The "avenue" is the channel between two rows of grapes. The "larder above your / head" is the bunches of grapes hanging from their vines over this channel.

By diminishing the perspective of the poem to that of the mouse, Moore reduces the power of her audience. It is partly human size that gives credence to human logic. While not the largest animals on earth, humans can stand up so that they lift themselves above other animals of their stature, both literally and figuratively. It is this stature that has been partially responsible for the human reliance on objectivity. We believe that we are more impressive than the animals over which we tower because of our size; we believe that we are better than animals that are larger than we are because of our intellects. Moore would take this power away from us to make us see that size and rationality are not essential qualities. Dadaists would agree with her action because of their belief that this human hubris brought about the First World War. In her quiet and professedly methodical way, Moore is adapting the radical fury of the dadaists to her poetry in order to expose the inherent fallacy behind an over-reliance on science and technology.

The end of this stanza asks a question about a picture of a mouse that is running with a grape in one "hand" and a baby in its mouth and that Moore saw in the February 1932 issue of *National Geographic Magazine*: "Does yonder mouse with a / grape in its hand and its child / in its mouth, not portray the Spanish fleece suspended by the neck?" (CP 17). Moore's assessment of this scene is enmeshed in her question whether it does not "portray / the Spanish fleece suspended by the neck." This statement must be ironic in intention. Spanish fleece would be a prized piece of shearling, yet the mouse baby is naked, wrinkled, and tiny. By introducing such a sarcastic tone into her scientific description of mouse behavior, Moore again aligns herself with the dada ambivalence about rationality and science; she admires rational method, yet she must always undercut it through her ultimate disapproval of it.

The sixth stanza of this poem turns the audience into the mouse through the use of the second person. Having addressed us as the mouse admiring its food, however, the poem shifts focus drastically to return us to human size, as a camera will move from a straight shot to a bird's-eye view. Now the poem describes the way the French take care of their table grapes while still on the vine, by putting them in a cage to give them the right amount of sun but protect them from the rain. This treatment of the grapes is a "pantomime of Persian thought" because the horticulturalists have become jewelers, taking care of their jewels; they are "gilded," "gems," "small pebble[s] of jade."

The perspective of the poem swings abruptly downward again, its dizziness meant to enhance Moore's refusal of constant objectivity. The seventh stanza returns to the mouse's view but to the mouse of fantasy, ridden by Tom Thumb, a rider who looks at the grapes from beneath in the flickering light that they allow to pass and who rides like a fury: "dashing around the *concours hippique* / of the tent, in a flurry / of eels, scallops, serpents, and other shadows from the blue of the green canopy" (CP 17–18). By leaving the world of realism entirely, the poet reveals her rejection of what gives that world meaning: rationalism, objectivity, and a belief in mimesis.

The poem's last stanza has to pull back to the poem's original topic to attempt to relate the grape to the camellia but yet at the same time to dismantle remaining scraps of logic. This stanza starts with a question, "The wine-cellar?" which means, Is this where these grapes will end up, as wine in bottles in storage? The answer is simple here: "No." The poem's reason for this answer is that making the grapes into wine "accomplishes nothing and makes the / soul heavy" (CP 18). Moore is surely not talking about her dislike of wine or drinking in general, though it is certainly a possibility given prohibition and her conservative tendencies. My impression is that the grape and what it provides for our table and for the inhabitants of the vineyard far outweigh the pleasures /benefits of what the grape becomes in wine. The "soul" becomes "heavy" at the thought of trampling these beautiful "jewels" which mean so much to the mouse.

This reading makes "the gleaning . . . more than the vintage" because it is what is left after the grape harvest that will tend the field animals. This horticulture for wine or for overly exotic flowers such as the camellia is fruitless.

Moore has taken on her highly moral tone in this stanza: "It accomplishes nothing" and "The gleaning is more than the vintage" (CP 18). This is in accord with the moral tendencies the dada movement expressed in its critical attitude toward the world that was falling apart around it. Moore uses this moral tone to appear to be making grand statements that explain human existence or dictate how people ought to behave. By minimizing the moral, however, she undermines the lesson of the fabular type in much the same way that the dadaists subverted themselves; by promoting chaos, each act of organization that they carried out (to hold a meeting, for instance) could only erode their very purpose.

The chaos of dada is apparent at the end of this poem. The plum has been considered a discrete species since 1797; the camellia does not like drafts, according to Abbé Berlèse; "O generous Bolzano!" Bolzano's generosity must be due to its less fussy attitude toward grapes and horticulture in general. Part of Moore's obliqueness here is due to her reluctance to be overtly critical, a similar dilemma facing those artists, particularly of Germany, who were under constant censorship surveillance. Just as Hannah Höch used photomontage to veil her disgust with Weimar Germany, Moore uses odd juxtapositions that disturb logical unity to conceal her sneering attitude toward the overemphasis that the French place on wine and food. In addition, the continual disruption of the dual play between Moore's scientifically objective language and her skeptical criticism of it in her description of the camellia's cultivation, in her description of the bottle of plums, reinforces her underlying distrust of too much attention paid to frivolous pastimes and of too much reliance on objectivity. Just as I will argue in my discussion of "The Jerboa," Moore critiques the materialism of the haute bourgeoisie in "Camellia Sabina" in favor of a more spiritually induced avant-garde art form. Here she expresses scorn for matters of "taste," "custom," "manners," and all that "haute cuisine" might signify in the life of the mediocre *petite bourgeoisie.*

"The Jerboa" reflects much of the same accordance with dada interest in technology, in critique of society and in reliance on randomness, but this poem provides an even clearer example of Moore's photomontage technique.[30] The images in "The Jerboa" are seemingly random; they require extensive explanation; they take on much of the antinarrative of the cubist in their lack of overt relation to one another. Yet, Moore uses this technique to criticize racism, the abuse of nature, and the entrapment that she had to endure of stifling bourgeois culture.

Gilbert and Schulze corroborate this reading of "The Jerboa." Gilbert argues, for instance, that, "seeking to imagine alternatives to the veracity and ferocity of history, the jerboa's celebrant strives to depict the alternative history that might be constructed" by using animals that represent Moore's value system.[31] Schulze, in comparing "The Plumet Basilisk" with "The Jerboa," says, "Menaced by restrictive and solidifying forces outside the self, both jerboa and basilisk jump into a self-protective poetry of faulty decorum meant to revise the oppressive tropes of detached and derivative romanticism."[32] These oppressive forces were, Gilbert says, based on "possession and enslavement, arrogance and ignorance," the hegemony, I believe, co-opted by the bourgeoisie.[33]

This poem is split into two sections: one with the heading "Too Much," the other entitled "Abundance," each of which follows with near-exact precision the six-line stanza with syllable patterns of 5, 5, 6, 11, 10, and 7 and a rhyme scheme of AABCDD. The titles of these two sections immediately proclaim Moore's moral tone by indicating the slight distinction between having enough, or having plenty for subsistence, and the tip over the edge from merely being comfortable into excess. Moore clearly disapproves of overmaterialism, of the overdomestication of nature that first the wealthy and then the bourgeoisie bring about.

She begins this poem with the enormous bronze cast of a pine cone that is currently owned by the Vatican but that was originally commissioned by one of the Pompeys. Moore's diction proclaims her dislike for human artifice:

> A Roman had an
> artist, a freedman,
> contrive a cone—pine-cone
> or fir-cone—with holes for a fountain. Placed on
> the Prison of St. Angelo, this cone
> of the Pompeys which is known
>
> now as the Popes', passed
> for art.
>
> (CP 10)

Moore's opprobrium for human interference with nature surfaces in the word "contrive," which indicates the need to cobble something together, that people cannot make pinecones as easily or as perfectly as pinetrees can. The very fact that it is unclear whether this tree is fir or pine bothers her—an ambiguity that nature would never tolerate. This cone has been ruined, furthermore, by having holes in it for water to spray through and out of it.

The most damning remark the poet makes, however, is that the bronze cast "passed for art." It isn't art; it isn't craft—it is merely what its audience "took" as art. This is the type of scornful criticism that the dadaists made toward the society that would blindly enter a disastrous war, that wouldn't question ethical issues, that denied intellectual aspirations.[34] By saying that the bronze cone passes for art, Moore sneers at the culture that would not understand what art is and that would take a poorly done representation of a naturally occurring object as art mainly because it is so large.

The rest of the first half of this poem becomes a list of the types of things people have done to nature, which takes in this poem the form of rendering the exotic into the domestic but which is really Moore's general criticism of the human destruction of animals, of human inappreciation of them. By extension, this moral tone evinces the blind quality of the bourgeoisie that would feel that nature is its playground, not its store of knowledge. Moore's dislike of this behavior is apparent in her subtle references. These people "used slaves"; "They had their men"; "They looked on as theirs" (meaning that Moore does not believe that these aspects of nature belong to men). These people put wild animals in gardens with artificially "square pools of pink flowers, tame fish, and small frogs." They gave "playthings" to boys, "such as / nests of eggs, ichneumon and snake, paddle / and raft, badger and camel" (CP 11). These odd pairings reflect Moore's disapproval; the idea that a badger and a camel would be good toys for a child, or an ichneumon and a snake, is farfetched and irresponsible.

The playthings that adults made for themselves are equally irresponsible:

> Lords and ladies put goose-grease
> paint in round bone boxes—the pivoting
> lid incised with a duck-wing
>
> or reverted duck-
> head; kept in a buck
> or rhinoceros horn,
> the ground horn; and locust oil in stone locusts.
>
> (CP 11)

The contents of these containers are odd derivatives from animals: paint made out of goose fat, oil distilled from locusts, aphrodisiacal powder ground from the rhinoceros horn. The containers themselves are in shapes appropriate to their contents: a locust for the locust oil, a horn for the rhinoceros horn powder, a duck-shaped box for the goose-fat paint.

Moore's tone here is ostensibly detached and descriptive, but her remark following this passage is sharply critical, revealing her disgust with these treatments of animals as decor. The phrase "It was a picture with a fine distance" ends with a semicolon that stops the poem abruptly but does not make sense grammatically because the next lines are only prepositional phrases. This technique induces a pause with a complementary image of the wealthy Romans and Egyptians as a well-made painting with passages into the far horizon. Because of her awkward drop into the prepositions, however, Moore undercuts this image; the next lines refer to drought and to the yearly swell of the Nile River.

Only the monkey and the dandy are present to watch the natural disasters occur. It is in her treatment of these two that Moore indicates her greater pleasure with the wild, naturally occurring animals and with those who take the time to observe. The "pig-tailed monkey on / slab-hands" has an "arched-up slack-slung gait" (CP 11). The repeated compound words quicken the reading of this section and articulate more finely the exact appearance of the monkey, more finely than the locust boxes or the horn receptacles. The dandy bears no description at all, other than his brown coloring, but what he looks at does ("the jasmine two-leafed twig / and bud, cactus-pads, and fig"), showing how much Moore approves of his action.

The rest of this first section of "The Jerboa" underscores Moore's disapproval of the wealthy who take advantage of the poor and who mistreat nature and natural phenomena. Moore conflates rewritten and fictional histories of the aristocratic eighteenth-century French, the Pharaonic Egyptians of the era immediately preceding and including Cheops, and the Romans of the times of Pompey, "those with, everywhere, / power over the poor" (CP 12). Moore believes that rulers of eras such as these only feel as keenly about their servants as about their *objets*; those who serve the rulers are "like the king's cane in the / form of a hand, or the folding bedroom / made for his mother of whom / / he was fond" (CP 12).[35] The excessive attention and energy directed toward these trivial possessions underscore the rulers' lack of esteem for human life or reasonable judgment about how relative importance should be assigned.

The scene that Moore depicts here strongly resembles the decadence of Marie Antoinette, who, with her ladies-in-waiting and courtiers, played at being shepherdesses and beekeepers at Trianon, but this version has the twist that the men dressed as women and the women as men, the men in "queens' dresses / calla or petunia / white, that trembled at the edge," and the women in "a / king's underskirt of fine-twilled thread like silk- / worm gut" (CP 12). Here, as with much of her poetic technique, Moore sets up a lovely scene, with light fabrics, sensitive to the breeze, out of refined silk, but then she disrupts this delicate fantasy with a word like "gut," which rips out the fantasy's viscera, displaying them for what they are—absurd.

Moore describes the pharaoh's fear of snakes in the third stanza from the end of this section as a segue into the next section of the poem. His fear induces him to tame the mongoose, a small animal who was not immortalized by a gigantic statue made in its likeness, "but there / was pleasure for the rat. Its restlessness was / its excellence; it was praised for its wit" (CP 12–13). Here Moore's critical attitude toward the earlier section of the poem becomes apparent through her evident relief and joy at turning to the jerboa, which is the main subject of her poem.[36]

This "desert rat" is "not famous," but it "has happiness," a contentment that Moore values far more than the wealth and energy of the kings that is spent on fruitless behavior. The repeated *s*'s, the exhilarated adjectives "stupendous" and "boundless," serve to reinforce Moore's pleasure with this small animal, which has "no ivory bed" like the queen's.

Having listed all that the jerboa does not have, water, trees, or bed, Moore seals this impression of approval for the rat by ending the first half of the poem with another aphoristic-sounding statement: "one would not be he / who has nothing but plenty." In this statement she expresses her disapproval of those who merely have a lot of anything but who have nothing useful to do with it, like the aristocracy. But the alternative to the aristocracy is the bourgeoisie. The French Revolution, for instance, was a revolution of the bourgeoisie. Moore is truly ambivalent about the bourgeoisie; they defeated the corrupt kings, so they were good, but they have little imagination and are overly materialistic, which was bad to Moore. This is similar to the disgust that the dadaists expressed concerning the First World War—at a time when technology could do so much and when people had energy to do so much, they were in fact using technology and the rationalizations of their so-called objectivity to waste their resources in an unforgivable manner.

Moore identifies this type of jerboa by its Saharan territory: "Africanus." She feels that Africanus is a misleading name: "It should mean the untouched" instead of "the conqueror sent / from Rome" (CP 13).[37] By wanting the jerboa to be identified as untouched, Moore asseverates her approbation that the jerboa has never been tamed by humans: "free-born." Moore comes back here, to the people who live in Africa, to reinforce her searing attack on racism against "the blacks, that choice race with an elegance / ignored by one's ignorance" (CP 13). Only those who know no better would miss the charm of this people.

Cristanne Miller devotes an entire chapter of her recent book to the issue of Marianne Moore and race. "Not surprisingly," Miller says, "Moore's concern with race is closely allied to her more general concerns with freedom and to her intense distrust of any system, institution, or structure that prejudges individual potential or worth."[38] Miller, however, criticizes Moore, I think justly, for depicting people of other races in a stereotypically and therefore potentially damaging manner. Miller says, for instance, that in "The Jerboa" Moore presents the nomadic Africans in the guise of the desert rat as "model[s] of morality, health, and satisfaction for those who live in middle- and upper-class exploitative decadence."[39] She is, therefore, behaving the way that Hollywood does when it represents Native Americans as uniformly tall, strong, and beautiful. Certainly there are some Native Americans like that, but the reality is far more complex than this representation would indicate.

Even so, Moore does her best to redress the injustice done to those lacking cultural power. She tries to show that life in the desert is not perfect. She acknowledges the threat that the desert presents in the form of mirages when she draws in the story of Jacob. The opponents whom Jacob meets, the "terrestrial" angel/wrestler and the "celestial" dreams and voices, come to him in the desert. "His friends were the stones" refers to his use of stones first as pillows and then, repeatedly, as pillars. These events were as mirages, though, "the translucent mistake / of the desert," in comparison to the mundane, yet practical, life of the jerboa. For the jerboa is not affected by mirages, either at rest or at intensest motion.

What is essential in this section of the poem is to understand what exactly Moore approves of in the appearance and behavior of the jerboa. Its body is designed for a type of movement particular to it and specially suited for the desert. It eats only to survive; it survives in the harshest of desert conditions. When this small desert jumping mouse moves, it moves with its body completely focused on leaping: "launching / as if on wings, from its match-thin hind legs, in / daytime or at night;[40] with the tail as a weight, / undulated out by speed, straight" (CP 14). The elaborate care of the rhymes and slant rhymes of this passage reflects Moore's exhilaration with the jerboa; "thin" to "hind" to "in," and "night" to "weight" to "straight," balanced by and tied to "daylight" in the next stanza, add speed to the length of the vowels.

The next three stanzas describe the jerboa in detail: the color and pattern of its fur, the shape of its body and head. Most of this description is simple, emphasized at times by the repeated pattern of *b*'s, finally relaxed in the pleasure of knowing that the markings of the body follow and emphasize its "contours."

The last part of the description changes in anticipation of the aphorism that concludes it: "strange detail of the simplified creature, / fish-shaped and silvered to steel by the force / of the large desert moon" (CP 14). The "strange detail" is the strong black-and-white marking at the end of the jerboa's tail. The rest of this animal has been streamlined for speed and toughened for desert life.

The aphorism itself, however, is another dada feature of this poem. This one is particularly strong: "Course / / the jerboa, or / plunder its food store, / and you will be cursed" (CP 14). This is the malediction with which Moore would have liked to have provoked those ancient rulers who would tame untamable animals to confine them to their gardens, who would interfere with the most practical appearances and behaviors of wild animals. This curse is also directed at those who would trammel human nature in ways that are overly restrictive. The ability to come and go as one chooses, as the jerboa does, to be unhunted or tampered with, would be a life unfettered by bourgeois confinements. As is typical with Moore, she stresses this point by cruising from "course" to "or" to "store," and then arresting this repetition of sound with the sharp finality of "curse," a searing condemnation of those who interfere.[41]

The rest of the poem, in fact, turns away from the scientific method of description into a lyrical depiction of the movements of the jerboa. This is an animal who is free, about whose freedom Moore is exuberant:

> By fifths and sevenths,
> in leaps of two lengths,
> like the uneven notes
> of the Bedouin flute, it stops its gleaning
> on little wheel castors, and makes fern-seed
> foot-prints with kangaroo speed.
>
> Its leaps should be set
> to the flageolet;
> pillar body erect
> on a three-cornered smooth-working Chippendale
> claw—propped on hind legs, and tail as third toe,
> between leaps to its burrow.
>
> (CP 14–15)

Moore emphasizes the double analogy of the jerboa's movement with musical tunes by using an irregular rhythm, yet one filled with double unstressed syllables, speeding up the poem, but retaining a hopping sensation.[42]

What is interesting about this second section of "The Jerboa," however, is Moore's reliance on features of machines and other technological inventions in her descriptions of this animal. The jerboa is "silvered to steel"; it is "on little wheel castors"; and the three points of its hind legs and tail create a "three-cornered smooth-working Chippendale / claw." To Moore, as to the dadaists, technology can explain nature and can, in fact, permit the same kind of pleasure that Moore finds in the jerboa. Moore and the other dadaists disdain too much tampering of the kind evidenced by the First World War or by the ancient rulers, but technology itself is a marvel.[43]

Heuving, Slatin, and Schulze remark with disapproval on the suddenly fixed final image.[44] Schulze, in particular, is scathing in her disappointment with Moore. She says that the jerboa transforms itself into the foot of a chair, "an immobile graven image of civilized society. Thus trapped, the quick 'fern-seed footprints' of the jerboa's verse become the solid, stylized feet of the British drawing room."[45] I agree with these critics that the ending of this poem is problematic, but I feel, as with "The Plumet Basilisk," that Moore feels compelled to withdraw from her furious critique.[46] Typical of the photomontage in this poem is the elusive quality of Moore's disapproval. She is on the surface merely expressing her distaste for ancient rulers' practices with animals and their servants and their pastimes; a deeper level of the poem, shown most explicitly through her aphorisms, reveals her extreme dislike of bourgeois convention and of overdomestication. The frozen posture of the jerboa at the end of the poem is at once a reflection of how a real animal would behave in danger and of how Moore feels about those—including, I believe, herself—who conform, those who become the model bourgeois immediately in the face of public opprobrium.

By submerging her already oblique moral statements of disapprobation for her culture, and by including equally moral statements on how culture ought to be instead, Moore embraces the photomontage of the Berlin dadaists. It is necessary to pry into her poems deeply and to investigate her sources in order to comprehend most clearly where her condemnation lies, just as it is essential with Höch's politically inspired photomontages to understand who her images were and why she approved or disapproved of them. This underlying critique/appreciation finally takes on more importance than the overall composition of the visual or verbal form, a composition weakened by time and by the loss of ready identification of its elements.

Two poems that carry this point further are two more of the group of Moore's "gardening" poems: "Radical" and "Injudicious Gardening." "Injudicious Gardening" first appeared as "To Browning" in *The Egoist* in 1915.[47] The revised versions of the poem, in *Observations* and *The Complete Poems*, indicate the extent to which Moore was trying to cover her tracks, as it were, as an avant-garde artist.

To understand this poem, it is important to go to Browning and his "square old yellow Book."[48] *The Ring and the Book* is an artistic rendering of scandalous events in Italy in 1697 and 1698, when Count Guido Franceschini of Arezzo married the thirteen-year-old Pompilia Comparini in order to improve his financial state. Guido treated Pompilia badly, she fled to her parents with the help of a young priest, and Guido had her and her family assassinated so that he could inherit their wealth through his child recently born to Pompilia. Browning recounts this history from the perspective of each of the main characters because, as he argues in the poem, "truth must prevail," and the way to get at the truth is through art and through composite perspectives.[49] Wylie Sypher argues that Browning's main themes in this poem are that truth is mutable and determined perspectively, and that personal actions based on individual ethics are far more important than those based on the status quo. Sypher contends, in fact, that "Browning scorns the accepted institutional values unless these values are held with a strongly personal sense of choice."[50] In the long run, then, while Browning valorizes Pompilia's independence of spirit, he yet sees truth as more balanced among disparate forces, "fixed, unchanging, and divinely ordained," according to Sypher.[51]

The color yellow in Moore's poem, then, refers to Browning's book, that little yellow book purporting to tell the truth and to get at this truth through the embellishment of art upon history. Moore's note on the poem refers us to the *Letters of Robert Browning and Elizabeth Barrett*: "The yellow rose? 'Infidelity,' says the dictionary of flowers." "I planted a full dozen more rose-trees, all white—to take away the yellow-rose approach."[52] Moore contends in this poem that gardening according to what colors might represent culturally is a mistake. I also believe, however, that the sense of the primacy of personal truth that Browning argues for in *The Ring and the Book* is foregrounded in the value system that this poem presents.

Moore takes further her opinion of the absurdity of gardening by color by saying that "if yellow betokens infidelity, / I am an infidel" (O 14). Infidelity usually refers to the unfaithful behavior of a spouse or lover; it occasionally can indicate treasonous behavior toward one's country. Infidelity never refers to religion, however. When the narrator says that she must be an "infidel" because she likes yellow roses, or because their color does not have an impact on her appreciation of them, she is using a word that is related to infidelity but that normally refers to a lack of faithfulness in the sense of participating in a religion, particularly a Christian one, given Moore's background. This wordplay exaggerates the importance of decisions about what to plant in one's garden, but this very exaggeration indicates the underlying seriousness of the issues that Moore is addressing in this poem.

The title of the poem also emphasizes this attack at the core of Moore's intentions. Gardening, like herding, is a term often used in descriptions of rulers. A well-ruled country, like a well-tended garden, repays the government in high levels of contentment and productivity. "Injudicious Gardening" would then refer to a leader who is unable to determine truth about situations, to balance the complexity of human behavior to come to decisions that make sense, to take sides on issues based on knowledge derived from stereotypes rather than from reality.

"However," the *Observation* version of the poem goes on, "your particular possession— / The sense of privacy / In what you did—deflects from your estate / Offending eyes, and will not tolerate / Effrontery" (O 14). The poem does not clarify its audience here. In the context of the original version of the poem, the "you" here probably refers to Browning, although given the second person voice in "Roses Only," there is some vagueness. Because Browning was wealthy enough to own a private estate, the change in his garden from yellow to white roses did not offend anyone because others could not see it. The implication here is that Moore does not have an estate—she has no privacy gained through immense wealth—and so she has no privacy of that kind to protect herself from prying eyes, from those who might criticize her behavior or beliefs. While Moore despises those watching her to the point of calling their treatment of her "effrontery," she still feels vulnerable to it.

When Moore revised this poem for *The Complete Poems*, she changed the second stanza to read:

However, your particular possession,
the sense of privacy,
indeed might deprecate
offended ears, and need not tolerate
effrontery.

(CP 81)

In some respects Moore radicalized this poem even further by these changes. She criticizes here not what Browning did—replacing yellow roses with white ones—but the very fact that he owns, "possesses," privacy, a feature of life open only to the very rich. In the *Observations* version of the poem, Browning's privacy protects him from public scrutiny and disapproval; the later version argues that the very fact of his privacy may make some people who hear about it upset. This later version, therefore, is much less protective of Browning and of his estate. It is possible, not to provide an overly biographical reading of this poem, that while Moore desired but did not have privacy in her earlier life, her mother being a constant presence, she yet felt criticism in her later life when her sense of private life was intact.

Browning's contention, then, that truth is a matter of context and perspective, plays into Moore's poem because of her criticism of the Brownings' (and the bourgeois middle-class as a whole) acceptance of stereotypical values, about colors in this case, but about beliefs in general. One's ethics are a matter of personal device, Moore argues, not one of embracing what cultural institutions offer without question.

The other gardening poem that I will discuss here as a dada-related work is "Radical." As with "Injudicious Gardening," in "Radical" Moore decries the oppression of the cultural critic, but in this case she finds solace in the irrepressible nature of the nonconformist. "Radical" first appeared in *Others* in 1919[53] and was included by Moore in *Observations* (O 48), but it was excluded by her in *The Complete Poems*. Of course, one very good reason for Moore's repression of this poem in the only volume of her work that is readily available is that she decided that it isn't a very good poem. The other reason, the one that I can only speculate about, is that she felt it was too overt in its culturally subversive message for her to allow it to remain in print.

Cultural subversion of this type appears in dada art, as in Man Ray's rayographs, a photographic process that denudes images of literal impact and divests art of spatial depth or progression. A rayograph in the

Museum of Modern Art's collection, for instance, depicts two heads facing each other and touching, just barely, at the lips. Superimposed upon these heads are the imprints of hands, one much brighter white than the other. A suggestion of smoke rises from the head of the left-hand image. The entire picture is blocked out with irregular rectangular shapes.

The process of the rayograph is simple. The artist starts with photographic paper and creates his image by exposing sections of the paper to varying exposures of light. The longer photographic paper is exposed to light, the darker it is after development (this makes the most sense when one considers that negatives present the reverse of their images).

The result of the rayograph is less simple, however, because the transparency of the images reduces the distinct quality of their original subjects. The heads, for instance, are clearly heads of people, but there are no apparent features that would determine their genders. A cultural transgression is occurring here, therefore, as gender is an essential mark in American culture whereby one's place is established.[54]

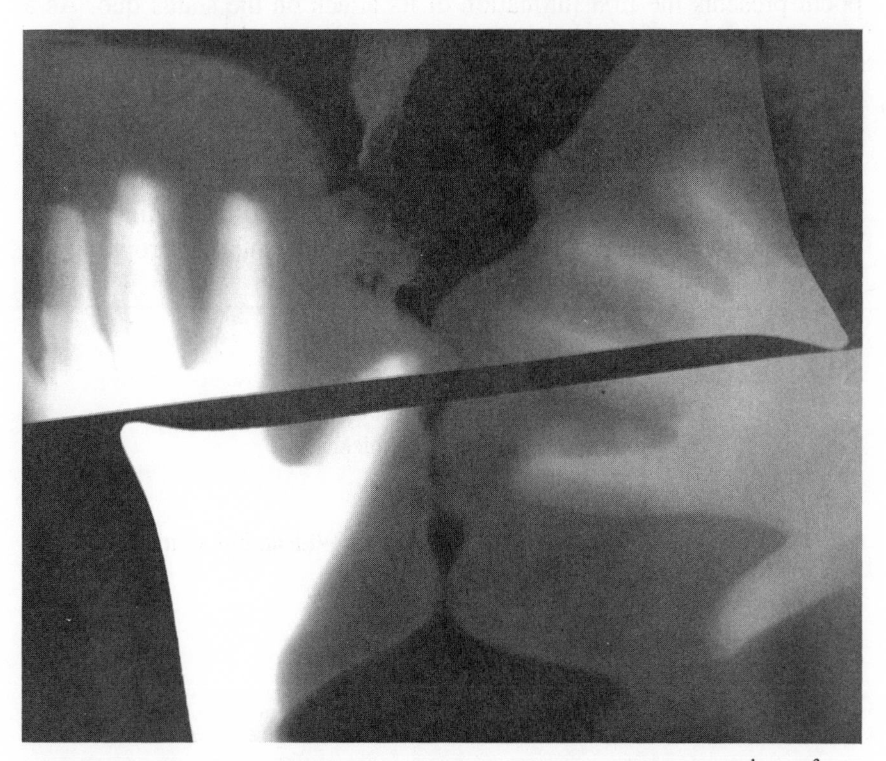

Man Ray (1890–1974). (Untitled), 1922. Gelatin-silver print (Rayograph), $9\frac{1}{2}$ X $11\frac{3}{4}$ in. The Museum of Modern Art, New York. Gift of James Thrall Soby (Photo: The Museum of Modern Art). © ARS.

Another transgressive feature of the rayograph involves its translucent quality. Because the outlines are indefinite and unfixed, and because the images seem to be so ephemeral, the rayograph disrupts the sense of progression from foreground to background in a different manner than photomontage does. Where photomontage places objects in direct juxtaposition, rayographs blur the lines between objects. The hands in this image seem to press into the heads and at once emerge out of them, rather than existing in separate or exclusive spheres. The softness of the outlines of the heads enhances this impression by creating the sense that they will at any minute merge into each other. The images, therefore, resist our impulse to read them as superimposed upon one another; instead, we see the entire image as in a state of flux, one which subverts cultural authority.

By presenting the modest and unassuming carrot as a culturally transgressive force in "Radical," Moore essentially performs the same artistic technique as Man Ray does in rayographs, through stretched enjambments, gross exaggeration, and frightening threats. The title alone of the poem presents the first intimation of its attack on the status quo. As a pun, the title reduces itself to a joke, but the subversive nature of the radical as extreme, as a proponent of revolution, is not superimposed by the radical as a root vegetable; instead, the two definitions lie side-by-side as a reenactment of Man Ray's irrepressible images that refuse to allow one to dominate, to lie closer to the foreground, than another.

Moore reinforces the humor and masking quality of this pun by using a comical rhyme scheme, forcing bizarre enjambments and dropping the ends of lines with heavy accents.

Radical

Tapering
to a point, conserving everything,
this carrot is predestined to be thick.
The world is
but a circumstance, a mis-
erable corn-patch for its feet. With ambition, imagination, outgrowth,

nutriment,
with everything crammed belligerent-
ly inside itself, its fibres breed mon-

opoly—
a tail-like, wedge-shaped engine with the
secret of expansion, fused with intensive heat to
color of the set-

ting sun and
stiff. For the man in the straw hat, standing still and turning to look back at it,
as much as
to say my happiest moment has
been funereal in comparison with this, the conditions of life pre-

determined
slavery to be easy and freedom hard. For
it? Dismiss
agrarian lore; it tells him this:
that which it is impossible to force, it is impossible
to hinder.

(O 48)

Moore starts this poem with a description of the carrot as protective of the existing order and resistant to change: "Tapering / to a point, conserving everything, / this carrot is predestined to be thick." The reversal at the end of this sentence undermines its ostensibly conformist character. The carrot does what it should, "tapers"; it doesn't waste anything or modify itself, it "conserves"; but if it follows this course, it will be "thick." Thick is a most unattractive adjective. As a physical characteristic, it describes an unappealing body; as an intellectual attribute, it refers to a lack of intelligence. The reversal in this line develops when Moore describes the good conservative citizen and then diminishes that description with such an unpleasant characteristic, reinforced by its placement both at the end of a sentence and at the end of a line.

The next line adopts a near-metaphysical conceit by connecting the humble life of the growing carrot to the entire earth: "The world is / but a circumstance, a mis- / erable corn-patch for its feet." The wild exaggeration of this passage subverts the stodgy and traditional bourgeois character, reinforced by the unlikely enjambments, especially the "mis-." Enjambments this improbable induce vibrations among possible endings. What can we expect here but "mis-take"? Instead, we get the "mis-chief" of misery, indicating the impoverishment, but also the sadness, the inferior quality, the inadequacy of the carrot's spot.[55]

This carrot deserves none of this "mis- / erable corn-patch," for it has "ambition, im- / agination, outgrowth, / nutriment." In a description of a carrot, "nutriment" makes sense, and so does "outgrowth" in its sense of growing outward, though not in its sense of consequence. Nor do "ambition" or "imagination" normally relate to a carrot, and these are qualities that are disapproved of in conventional society, where conformism is the norm. Again, the amusement that this description of a carrot engenders cannot camouflage the serious intensity of the underlying message, of Moore's approval of the qualities of ambition and imagination. Here, too, the irregular enjambment of "im- / agination" reinforces this reading. The "im-" could be finished with imperative, the idea of cultural control or force, for instance, but it instead ends with "agination," giving it a culturally subversive quality, as imagination is suspect because nonconformist, but also reverberating with the activity of the similar word, "agitation."

The hostility of the poem toward conformism strikes the surface in this stanza through forcefully aggressive language and powerful machines. These attributes of the carrot do not exist peacefully within its walls; they are "crammed belligerent- / ly inside itself." This carrot is suddenly a monster. It has uncontrollable energy driving it through the ground, an "engine with the secret of expansion." As with "The Jerboa" and "Camellia Sabina," the fascination of the dadaists with technology enters into Moore's work.

Moore's ambivalence with technology surfaces here, too, however, in the fear of this puissant phallus, through her language from economics of "monopoly," an unapproved business practice; through her language from biology of "breed," an unattractive description for reproduction;[56] through her language from physics of "fused with intensive heat," a covert reference to the crushing power of the sun. Moreover, this carrot is a phallus, a disturbing image to Moore, for it is "stiff," but also a subversive reference to sex for one who claims to be so modest and inexperienced. Once again, the enjambment sets off this word to emphasize it, as does the awkward grammatical structure because the "engine" is "fused" and "stiff." Moore conceals the word somewhat, though, by setting it well inside the line rather than at its end, like "thick."

The perspective of the poem shifts completely at this moment because a man is suddenly present—the farmer—much pleased with his lowly object of cultivation. This man presents the principle of the poem by thinking that "the conditions of life pre- / / determined / slavery to be easy and freedom hard." He sees the carrot as in a good position, trapped in the soil, because the options of personal choice and the ability to act as one pleases would create more difficult lives for us.

Inevitably, though, the man must accept that he cannot constrain the carrot in bondage: "that which it is impossible to force, it is impossible / to hinder." He has no power over the carrot once he has planted it. He can't make it grow in a particular way; nor can he prevent it from growing, short of picking it before its time. The earlier depiction of the carrot as a juggernaut feeds into this final statement. This "machine" will do what it wants, unaffected by constraints of social expectations.

Just as Schulze sees "The Jerboa" as a self-portrait by Moore, I see "Radical" as another. She is the nonconformist struggling with constrictive social conventions; she is the furiously energetic phallus striving to reject social repression. She is the poetic force that "it is impossible to hinder." She looks modest, like the carrot, with her red hair, but she contains within her the power of subversion like the carrot's power to drive into the earth.

As with Höch, however, Moore felt unable to rebel from the status quo, partly, as I have suggested, because her ambivalence was genuine: she felt compelled to criticize, for she suffered under its stifling convention, yet she at the same time had a strong investment in the culture of the American bourgeoisie. This conflict led her to devise a poetry similar in focus to the technique of photomontage, with its delight in technology and its strong juxtaposition of disparate images, but also with its skill at masking its underlying intention. Like Man Ray, Moore flouted perspectival traditions, too, by taking an overlooked root, normally receded into the background, and displaying it with such force that the foreground and background of this poem merge.

Afterword: Marianne Moore's Surrealism: "Mystery is a convenient cloak for the unpermissable"

When it comes to surrealism, unlike the other arts movements of the earlier part of the twentieth century, literature, especially the literature of poetry, feeds the visual arts. This reversal of the flow, as it were, is no surprise, given that the major figures of the surrealist movement in France were writers: André Breton, Louis Aragon, Philippe Soupault, Robert Desnos, and Paul Eluard.[1] The manifestos that Breton and Aragon, among others, wrote shaped the direction of the corresponding visual arts movement.

As with the preceding art movements discussed in this book, surrealism maintained a strong degree of subversion, but to a quite different end. Instead of attempting to undermine the establishment directly, the surrealists desired to unify the separated artistic strands of aestheticism and political engagement by conjoining the two wildly divorced worlds of reality and dream. Walter Benjamin enhanced this goal by equating the world of dreams with the realm of history and by arguing that the unconscious reveals itself through study of the past just as much as it does through examination of dreams.

Benjamin's project focused on the city as the site of the barrier between the past and the present, as to other surrealists the moment of awakening is the barrier between the dreaming state and the conscious one. In her poems of cities, but also of place, Moore adapted the poem to the surrealist agenda by using the poem itself as the line of demarcation between appearances and underlying explanations for these appearances that are repressed by the culture. By looking at two of Moore's poems, "New York" and "People's Surroundings," I would like to place her works as essentially surrealist in nature as they investigate this very interface between what a culture acknowledges and what it withholds.

Both Breton and Moore overtly emphasize the literary in surrealism. Moore wrote a review of a 1937 art show at the Museum of Modern Art, whose curators suggested that surrealism had its antecedents in earlier art by such artists as Hieronymus Bosch, Giuseppe Arcimboldo, and William Hogarth. She mentions several times in this article that the visual artists were using literary techniques to depict their subjects by way of surrealism: "Throughout the rooms, one felt the tendency to multiple thinking; that is to say, the prevalence of innuendo and humor, effected often by paradox and the pun. As in books, these two literary devices work for or against the product . . . cheapening or tending to a dazzling compactness."[2] Breton confirms this emphasis on the literary in surrealism by arguing that "whoever speaks of expression speaks of language first and foremost. It should therefore come as no surprise to anyone to see surrealism almost exclusively concerned with the question of language at first, nor should it surprise anyone to see it return to language."[3]

Breton identified surrealism as "psychic automation in its pure state, by which one proposes to express—verbally, by means of the written word, or in any other manner—the actual functioning of thought. Dictated by thought, in the absence of any control exercised by reason, exempt from any aesthetic or moral concern." He goes on to describe the philosophy of this movement as being "based on the belief in the superior reality of certain forms of previously neglected associations, in the omnipotence of dream, in the disinterested play of thought."[4] In this manifesto of surrealism, Breton argues, therefore, against standards set by bourgeois culture to determine actions or beliefs on the basis of "reason," "morality," and "aesthetics," aesthetics and morality that are set by cultural directives.

Breton emphasizes the cultural subversion of surrealism in his manifestos by complaining that "we are still living in the reign of logic," and "the absolute rationalism that is still in vogue allows us to consider only facts relating directly to our experience," excluding the fuller reality, the "surreality," which represents our selves at their most complete.[5]

In "Surrealism: The Last Snapshot of the European Intelligentsia," Walter Benjamin relates this subversive character of surrealism to its deep immersion in political activism, but he also identifies the extent to which surrealism drew on issues of aestheticism. He describes Breton's philosophy by saying that the poet had the "intention of breaking with a praxis that presents the public with the literary precipitate of a certain form of existence while withholding that existence itself."[6] Aestheticism, as an art movement, withdrew from practical experience. Art, in the bourgeois mentality, had no logical or rational function and was therefore to be relegated to a sphere outside the practical, denuded of influence or power.[7]

However, the surrealists fought against the isolation of art and strove to draw it directly into a role as politically active. Benjamin identifies this effort by saying, "In the transformation of a highly contemplative attitude into revolutionary opposition, the hostility of the bourgeoisie toward every manifestation of radical intellectual freedom played a leading part."[8] The surrealists, therefore, redirected the artistic goals of aestheticism by politicizing it and thereby setting it against the strictures of bourgeois culture.[9]

Breton's theory of surrealism relies heavily on Freudian explanations of the operations of the subconscious, as is evidenced by references to Freud in his manifestos. Freud contended that in order to achieve some sense of one's real self, it is essential to scan for sites of repression and to endeavor to remove them to reveal the originary person within each of us.[10] There were two main methods for reaching this sense of reality: through the analysis of dreams and through free association, the seemingly random expression of surfacing thoughts that hopefully identify sites of repression.

The surrealists relied on both of these techniques. They tried automatic writing, but while they certainly looked at dreams as the mirror of reality, they focused their attention on the barrier between the waking and dreaming states as the moment when we are truly unified.[11] Since it is seemingly impossible to achieve this sense of reality, the surrealists tried to see and understand dreams in the waking state. John McCole identifies this effort by saying: "The shimmer of mystery surrounding ordinary objects and places as the surrealists experienced them . . . was a modern trace to this archaic form of experience."[12] Yet, for Marianne Moore, this mystery is essential, for, as the quotation in the title of this chapter indicates, mystery is also useful in masking one's true intent.[13]

It is not a very great leap from the surrealists' view of dreams to

Benjamin's view of history, for dreams contain elements of our past in them, whether from the previous day's events or from events that occurred in a more distantly past time.[14] What the surrealists were doing, according to Benjamin, was developing a "mythic consciousness"; myth was, as Aragon wrote, the "conveyor belt" of consciousness and was, therefore, the route to an understanding of, a revelation of, reality or surreality.[15]

To Benjamin, the city was a "labyrinth," the intricate and seemingly random design of which parallels the conscious.[16] By deciphering the historical roots of the city, what composed it into the form in which it currently exists, it should be possible to discern the shape of the cultural conscious in the same way that the elements of the past appearing in dreamform identify to a certain degree the individual consciousness. "The dialectical interpenetration and making-present of past contexts," Benjamin argues, "is the test of the truth of present action."[17] Only by looking at the past and at its influence upon the present, its shaping of the present, can we determine the consistency of the present. Only by looking at the past can we reveal the unconscious of the present, blocked (repressed) by the intervention of memory.

In "New York" and "People's Surroundings," Moore creates a myth of consciousness, "New York," in much the same way that Benjamin describes, by seeing the city as a labyrinth composed of elements of its past that percolate into and mold the present. Leavell identifies the mythic elements of this poem, but with reservations about Moore's presentation of them:

> On the one hand is America's idealized noble "savage" suggested by teepees (New York Indians never lived in teepees), war canoes, and Indian geographical names; on the other is the savagery of commerce plundering the state's bountiful resources. . . . This is then the paradoxical "savage's romance": to romanticize the savage is itself savage.[18]

Moore, with her attention to veracity, both scientific and historical, certainly knew that the New York Indians did not live in teepees. This view of the Indians creates, though she scoffs at it, an American myth of its past similar to those of James Fenimore Cooper. Our ability to see into the past is hindered by the incomplete and inaccurate operations of our memories, memories that create a history different from the actual one. It was Benjamin's project to attempt to pierce this barrier between the present and the past in order to achieve a state of reality; it was Moore's project as well.

Moore has a vision in this poem of Manhattan Island before Wall Street took over, but her description of the Native Americans represents the bountiful view of the wilderness, so teeming with furred animals that the Indians' life was plush and warm from their pelts:

> starred with tepees of ermine and peopled
> with foxes,
> the long guard-hairs waving two inches beyond
> the body of the pelt;
> The ground dotted with deer-skins—white
> with white spots
> "as satin needlework in a single color may
> carry a varied pattern,"
> and wilting eagles' down compacted by the
> wind;
> and picardels of beaver skin; white ones
> alert with snow.
>
> (O 65)

Of course this description is exaggerated, but wildly enough to draw a contrast with what has replaced a civilization that has not repressed its past or its consciousness, a contrast that Moore draws directly by comparing the perfection of life in this pristine nirvana to the overwrought and decadent New York of the early twentieth century:[19]

> It is a far cry from the "queen full of
> jewels"
> and the beau with the muff,
> from the gilt coach shaped like a perfume
> bottle,
> to the conjunction of the Monongahela and the
> Allegheny, and the scholastic philosophy of
> the wilderness
> to combat which one must stand outside and
> laugh
> since to go in is to be lost.
>
> (O 65)

These last two lines do not appear in the version of this poem published in Moore's *Complete Poems*. She took them out, I believe, because they state too clearly how much the wilderness represents the unfathomable unconscious; how scary it is to us, how labyrinthine it is in nature, but also how much she feels the compulsion to face it herself and how drawn she is to it.

The last section of the poem devolves into a series of negative constructions that, as Miller points out, make Moore sound overtly "contentious."[20] She repeats "It is not" four times before getting to what it is. The pronoun "it" has no clear referent either. It might refer to New York itself; it might replace "the savage's romance." It must, however, refer to the reality that the surrealists were trying to reach and comprehend, for this subject lies between the world of materialism and the world of fantasy: "It is not the dime-novel exterior" or the lavishness of furs or the ability to trap animals or the desire to make money off of them: "it is the 'accessibility to experience.'"

The "it," then, represents the desire to look for true history, to decipher the real past in the relics whose traces it leaves in the present in order to understand the present more fully. The "'accessibility to experience,'" a quotation from Henry James, indicates that Moore is arguing that, instead of relying on culturally manufactured meaning and readings of the past, we need to look clearly at what we see going on now as a way to comprehend the true past more fully.[21] She is also suggesting that the present preoccupation with the material, with the quality of one's fur or the design of one's jewelry, is equally artificially determined, that the way to see life is to see it based on one's direct experience with it.

Marianne Moore took Benjamin's theory of the city one step further in "People's Surroundings" by looking at the objects that we select to have around us as the entrance into the labyrinth of our idiosyncratic pasts. "They answer one's questions"—the "they" is these objects, these artifacts, which combined, depict the individual; they are the intersection between the past and the present.

Heuving refers to this poem as one of Moore's "list" poems.[22] If a surrealist is trying to interpret this intersection between the conscious and the unconscious, whether via the interpretation of dreams, free association, automatic writing, or historical representations in the present, lists are guaranteed to be the end result.[23] It is by sifting through these seemingly random lists that the hoped-for apprehension of the surreality, of the complete reality, for which the surrealists are striving, can be accomplished. This is why, as Heuving says, "Moore enlarges the definition of 'surroundings' to include historical and psychological factors and subverts the values and associations attached to such dualities as surface and depth, and commerce and culture."[24] Moore is looking for the complete assessment of character, of the surreality of the individual, and, therefore, must pose as features of this character all the possible influences that bring its composition to bear, including, in particular, artifacts of memory.

In composing this list, however, Moore clarifies what character should be like: the "deal table compact with the wall" is perfect—"one's style is not lost in such simplicity" (O 66–68).[25] Bad character is revealed in "bad furniture," including the "vast indestructible necropolis / of composite Yawman-Erbe separable units."[26] The essential problem that Moore has with this type of "furniture" is its generally impractical value—she desires always to unify practicality with aesthetic taste. The Poor Richard publication, then, fails because while it proclaims the bourgeois standards of behavior—"efficient" and materialistic—the extreme thinness of the paper on which it is printed may save a few trees, but it is essentially inutile because it is unreadable. The fact that the pamphlet contains "public secrets" emphasizes this paradox: secrets that have been published are no longer secret, but if those secrets are published in an unreadable form they remain unknown.

The mention of time here reinforces this stress on efficiency: "When you take my time, you take / something I had meant to use" (O 66). Time is an essential quantity to the follower of the Protestant work ethic, the waste of which the Poor Richard author would have found immoral. The author's tone here is of essence; the dry and ironic humor expressed through exaggeration and odd juxtapositions (the book and the microscope, for instance) denote the undermining and therefore critical nature of the expression.

The next stanza dives deeply into the labyrinth of human decorative folly: shadows, hidden features, elaborate gates, mirrored by the intricate lacing of the tree shadows, mirrored once again by the "twisted" maze of the garden. These are features of human production that are not valued by the author.

By contrast, and equally unappealing to Moore, is the lack of imagination, the "straight" mind, where roads never bend, where people rely on "common sense" and have a laconic forecast of the unknown future: "they can like trout, smell what is coming." When Moore announces,

"There is something attractive about a mind that moves in a straight line," she seems to appreciate it, but in her list of what this kind of mind does, select "concrete statuary" and build "the municipal bat-roost of mosquito warfare," her disapproval is evident. The *Complete Poems* version of this stanza ends with, "These are questions more than answers," indicating that, as there is no definite approach to solving the surrealist dilemma, Moore may at least establish what is indefinite to her and what does not represent a solution (CP 56).

The sixth stanza of this poem leaves America entirely and flies to the Caribbean with "Bluebeard's tower above the coral reefs." The colors, the intensity of the language (even for poetry), the sparkle and glitter, the wild array of sights, recall Wallace Stevens's "Sunday Morning" and evoke a similar message: the beauty of the dream transcends this world and takes the traveller closer to a sense of what has been repressed into the unconscious. The dream, however, as I have mentioned, is not the surrealist goal but rather goes beyond reality without explaining it.

Therefore, as Moore ends this stanza, it is impossible to attain this "intoxication" that Benjamin proposes for the surrealists:[27] "the mind of this establishment has come to the conclusion / that it would be impossible to revolve about one's self too much, / sophistication has like 'an escalator,' 'cut the nerve of progress'" (O 68). The power of the status quo, the "establishment," dictates that feeling, particularly of the type of passion expressed by this dream, would be inappropriate. It is also not proper to spend too much time dwelling on "one's self"; bourgeois practice indicates that the external world rules to the neglect of the internal one.

So, the polite person of society sees the objects, tangible or intangible, which circle the individual and understands the etiquette that requires that we never look too closely or get too personal: "The physiognomy of conduct must not reveal the skeleton" (O 68). Yet it is impossible to avoid seeing beneath the surfaces, to ignore the past influences on the present, or the infrastructure on the structure: "Yet with x-raylike inquisitive intensity upon it, the surfaces go back. . . . We see the exterior and the fundamental structure" (O 68).

Moore ends this poem with a list drawn from real life, this time of the people and things that make contemporary industrial life what it is: people of all ranks of life and all professions, places of all kinds where they work and of all types of habitations. While the fantasy of the tropics is appealing, it can't possibly reveal the consciousness that is the goal of the surrealist; it is by examining normal life and normal possessions that this potential may perhaps be fulfilled.

Slatin argues that this poem fails to develop the community that Moore so urgently requires, and that she only succeeds in realizing that "the contemporary world through which the first sentence passes is dead . . . because . . . it is indifferent to 'the fundamental structure,' the immanent past."[28] I contend instead that in fact it is because Moore sees the past in the present that she can use the tools and goals of surrealism to effect her own goal of seeing the conscious in the labyrinth of the artifacts surrounding us.

Moore's purpose in many of her poems, therefore, is to develop through abstraction and montage a sense of individual and cultural subjectivity. By exposing camouflaged structures of culture through the accretion in her poetry of natural and aesthetic productions, Moore can reveal to us the influence of tradition and history in order to promote social and cultural change away from inherent restrictions and inconsistencies. Because of her adaptation of contemporary art movements, Moore was able to critique inadequacies in her own culture, those ranging from mere irritations to seriously repressive cultural standards. By doing so, she firmly enmeshed herself in the avant-garde agenda, to reunite political activism with the esthetic goals of the visual arts. As an avant-garde artist, she freely used collage, montage, cubistic fracturing, and surrealist illogic in order to shield herself from cultural opprobrium by masking the critical nature of her principles through abstraction, while promoting cultural adjustments to its own inadequacies.

Notes

Introduction

1. Charles Molesworth, *Marianne Moore: A Literary Life* (New York: Atheneum, 1990), 427–33.

2. See the interviews with Hall and Schulman in Donald Hall, *Marianne Moore: The Cage and the Animal* (New York: Pegasus, 1970) and Grace Schulman, *Marianne Moore: The Poetry of Engagement* (Urbana: University of Illinois Press, 1986). On self-effacement, see Cristanne Miller, *Marianne Moore: Questions of Authority* (Cambridge: Harvard University Press, 1995), and Sandra Gilbert and Susan Gubar, *Mad Woman in the Attic* (New Haven: Yale University Press, 1980), 541–49.

3. Schulman, 159.

4. Betsy Erkkila, *The Wicked Sisters: Women Poets, Literary History and Discord* (Oxford: Oxford University Press, 1992), 102–4; Cynthia Hogue, *Scheming Women: Poetry, Privilege and the Politics of Subjectivity* (Albany: SUNY Press, 1995), 73. Carolyn Durham points out that "Moore's poetry uses a nineteenth-century strategy of the double text to announce the themes and techniques that become overt in modernist and postmodernist women's poetry: an apparent renunciation of self overlays the subversive encoding of female sexuality; an apparently gender-free concern with linguistic and formal experimentation conceals the subversive rejection of male language" ("Linguistic and Sexual Engendering in Marianne Moore's Poetry," in *Engendering the Word: Feminist Essays in Psychosexual Poetics*, ed. Temma F. Berg [Urbana: University of Illinois Press, 1989], 225).

5. See Gilbert and Hogue on Moore's appearance, especially on her cross-dressing. Sandra Gilbert, "Marianne Moore as Female Female Impersonator," in *Marianne Moore: The Art of a Modernist*, ed. Joseph Parisi (Ann Arbor: University of Michigan Press, 1990), 27–46.

6. Lisa Steinman, "'So As to Be One Having Some Way of Being One Having Some Way of Working': Marianne Moore and Literary Tradition," in *Gendered Modernisms: American Women Poets and Their Readers*, ed. Margaret Dickie and Thomas Travisano (Philadelphia: University of Pennsylvania Press, 1996), 97–116; Linda Leavell, *Marianne Moore and the Visual Arts: Prismatic Color* (Baton Rouge: Louisiana State University Press, 1995). Leavell's extensive primary research on Moore's relation to the visual arts is an invaluable source for this study.

7. Steinman, 100.

8. Jacques Derrida, *The Truth in Painting*, trans. Geoff Bennington and Ian McLeod (Chicago: University of Chicago Press, 1987), 22.

9. Ibid., 61.

10. Miller uses the work of Ross Chambers to suggest that Moore's poetry represents "oppositional behavior," which in order to contest social practices must also adhere to them (8–9); Carolyn Burke, "Getting Spliced: Modernism and Sexual Difference," *American Quarterly* 39.1 (spring 1987): 102; Jeanne Heuving, *Gender in the Art of Marianne Moore: Omissions Are Not Accidents* (Detroit: Wayne State University Press, 1992), 27.

11. Nancy Fraser is critical of Julia Kristeva on this issue because Kristeva contends that only art is transgressive ("The Uses and Abuses of French Discourse Theory," in *Revaluing French Feminism: Critical Essays on Difference, Agency, & Culture*, ed. Nancy Fraser and Sandra Lee Bartky [Bloomington: Indiana University Press, 1992], 187). I agree with Fraser—other aspects of any culture are equally transgressive and/or desirous of change as the arts. The transgression of the arts of the early twentieth century, however, is more easily discernable than other parts of the culture, though not all, and therefore relatively easy to study. Note Martin Green's *New York 1913,* which examines the art of the time but also the convulsions present in labor unions (*New York 1913: The Armory Show and the Paterson Strike Pageant* [New York: Scribners, 1988]).

12. Whether starting an assessment of this debate with Lessing's disapproval of the relations between the arts (visual=spatial; verbal=temporal), or with Norman Bryson's contemporary version of semiotics, or Charles Altieri's application of Wittgensteinian agency, an excellent overview for the history of the argument about literature and the visual arts is in Marianna Torgovnik's introduction to *The Visual Arts, Pictorialism and the Novel: James, Lawrence and Woolf* (Princeton: Princeton University Press, 1985).

13. See W. J. T. Mitchell, *Iconology: Image, Text, Ideology* (Chicago: University of Chicago Press, 1986): "The distinctive modernist emphasis is on the image as a sort of crystalline structure, a dynamic patterning of the intellectual and emotional energy bodied forth by a poem. Formalist criticism is both a poetics and a hermeneutics for this kind of verbal image, showing us how poems contain their energies in matrices of architectonic tension, and demonstrating the congruence of these matrices with the propositional content of the poem" (25).

14. As a way to illustrate the revitalization of older, disused critical approaches, see Marshall Sahlins's structuralism in his studies of Hawaii at the time of Captain Cook's visits (*How "natives" think: about Captain Cook, for example* [Chicago: University of Chicago Press, 1995]). Instead of depicting, as if in crystalline form, the operations of a culture at a fixed moment in time, Sahlins uses the technique of determining cultural structure to study points and instances of cultural change.

15. Fraser argues convincingly in "The Uses and Abuses of French Discourse Theory" that "by reducing discourse to a 'symbolic system,' the structuralist model evacuates social agency, social conflict, and social practice" (181). Lee Paterson reinforces this concern in his discussion of New Historicism by expressing his fears that "the focus on culture as semiosis can induce the literary mind to occlude the material entirely. The effect is to return to a wholly textualized history, in which acts have symbolic significance but no practical consequences, in which history consists of gestures rather than real actions" ("Literary History," in *Critical Terms for Literary Study*, 2nd ed., ed. Frank Lentricchia and Thomas McLaughlin [Chicago: University of Chicago Press, 1995], 261).

Semiotics can be useful in interart studies, as Steiner's work demonstrates, but it, like formalism, needs to be used with extreme care to avoid a view of culture as calcified.

16. Ann Jefferson, "Literariness, Dominance and Violence in Formalist Aesthetics," in *Literary Theory Today*, ed. Peter Collier and Helga Geyer-Ryan (Ithaca: Cornell University Press, 1990), 125–41.

17. Fraser, 185.

18. Mikhail M. Bakhtin, *The Dialogic Imagination*, ed. Michael Holquist, trans. Caryl Emerson and Michael Holquist (Austin: University of Texas Press, 1981), 276.

19. Bakhtin, in fact, dismisses the ability of poetic language to engage in its environment because the word in poetry is too deeply involved with itself and with the interaction that it has with the other words in the poem and with the creation of images of which it is a part (278). I argue that poetry, certainly at the very least, the poetry of Marianne Moore, is deeply invested in an interaction with its own culture, at once in support of and in critique of it. Contemporary critics of Moore's work use the word "transgression" with frequency, indicating their adherence to pragmatic discourse theory. (See Leigh Gilmore, "The Gaze of the Other Woman: Beholding and Begetting in Dickinson, Moore, and Rich," in *Engendering the Word: Feminist Essays in Psychosexual Poetics*, ed. Temma F. Berg (Urbana: University of Illinois Press, 1989): "transgression as the privileged form of self-assertion" (82); "women . . . transgress . . . against a narrative that would prohibit their potential enchantment" (99). See, too, Miller (5) and Hogue (83).

20. For detailed descriptions of Moore's biographical relations to the visual arts, see Heuving and Bonnie Costello (*Marianne Moore: Imaginary Possessions* [Cambridge: Harvard University, 1981]), among others.

21. See Rachel Blau DuPlessis on satire and parody, both of which, while critical of their subjects, also express admiration for them ("'Corpses of Poesy': Some Modern Poets and Some Gender Ideologies of Lyric," in *Feminist Measures: Soundings in Poetry and Theory*, ed. Lynn Keller and Cristanne Miller [Ann Arbor: University of Michigan Press, 1994], 69–95).

22. In a discussion of abstraction in modernist poetry, it is necessary to address Charles Altieri's (as well as Wendy Steiner's) theory of iconicity (Charles Altieri, *Painterly Abstraction in Modernist Poetry: The Contemporaneity of Modernism* [Cambridge: Cambridge University Press, 1989]; and Wendy Steiner, *Exact Resemblance to Exact Resemblance: The Literary Portraiture of Gertrude Stein* [New Haven: Yale University Press, 1978]). Altieri feels that iconicity replaces representation in modern art, that "intentional agency changes so that representation becomes not a representation of a scene, object, or person, *per se*, but of a state. . . . Art is not interpretation of experience, but a pure state" (38). The importance here is not that Moore's poetry becomes so self-referential that it loses even the type of abstract iconicity that Altieri describes, but that she is representing the same types of ideas and principles that the romantic poets did (I am using them as a ground here, only because Altieri does). It is not that the idea of representation has changed for modern poets: how ideas are represented has changed; what ideas are represented has changed; but that they are presented at all has not. See chapter 1 in this book for more on iconicity.

23. Moore's poetry, as every critic who writes on her complains, is difficult to address because of the lack of a complete collection of her work and because of her habit of constant revision. I am using the 1924 *Observations* for the most part, though I turn to

The Complete Poems of Marianne Moore where needed by the argument at hand. Many more studies need to be done like Robin Gail Schulze's on the effects of revisions on Moore's poems (see "'The Frigate Pelican''s Progress: Marianne Moore's Multiple Versions and Modernist Practice," in *Gendered Modernisms: American Women Poets and Their Readers*, ed. Margaret Dickie and Thomas Travisano [Philadelphia: University of Pennsylvania Press, 1996], 117–39).

Chapter 1. The Veil of Abstraction: Cultural Critique and the Imagination

1. The New York dada scene was, by American standards, highly radical. These artists, by rejecting normative modes of artistic production, expressed their denial of representative tradition and embraced the political. See Serge Guilbaut, *How New York Stole the Idea of Modern Art: Abstract Expressionism, Freedom, and the Cold War*, trans. Arthur Goldhammer (Chicago: University of Chicago Press, 1983).

2. This is the title under which this painting is currently designated at the Philadelphia Museum of Art. "Curious splinter salad" was the phrase used by the contemporary reviewer Adeline Adams in "The Secret of Life," *Art and Progress* 4 (April 1913): 931.

3. Anna C. Chave's article on Picasso's *Les Desmoiselles d'Avignon* presents this idea in detail ("New Encounters with *Les Demoiselles D'Avignon*: Gender, Race, and the Origins of Cubism," *The Art Bulletin* 76 [December 1994]: 596–611).

4. This sets up an interesting relation between painting and film, in terms of theories of voyeurism and objectification of the static object such as that laid out by Laura Mulvey in "Visual Pleasure and Narrative Cinema," *Screen* 16.3 (autumn 1975): 6–18.

5. C. Bernheimer notes that "from the mid-nineteenth century to the beginning of the twentieth, modernism obsessively and anxiously displays its innovative desire by fragmenting and disfiguring the female sexual body" (*Figures of Ill Repute: Representing Prostitutes in Nineteenth-Century France* [Cambridge: Harvard University Press, 1989], 266). This trend is apparent in such poems by William Carlos Williams as "Queen Anne's Lace" and "Portrait of a Lady." Benjamin H. D. Buchloh also comments on "the abandonment of painting as sexual metaphor, [which] implied not only formal and aesthetic changes but also a critique of traditional models of sublimation" ("Figures of Authority, Ciphers of Regression: Notes on the Return of Representation in European Painting," *October* 16 [spring 1981]: 58).

6. Taffy Martin's work on Moore has been a notable exception here (*Marianne Moore: Subversive Modernist* [Austin: University of Texas Press, 1986]).

7. Hogue, 108–9.

8. Miller, 34–35. Other works that have recently been published on Moore's work and that depict her as an innovative and strong poet include Durham; Robin Gail Schulze, *The Web of Friendship: Marianne Moore and Wallace Stevens* (Ann Arbor: University of Michigan Press, 1995); Margaret Holley, *The Poetry of Marianne Moore: A Study in Voice and Value* (Cambridge: Cambridge University Press, 1987); and Heuving.

9. Martin would disagree with my point here, as she contends that Moore is a "renegade within the context of high modernism" (56). I believe that Moore's work is too socially and politically engaged to suit the high modernist label.

10. Peter Bürger, in fact, says that "Lukacs's and Adorno's avoidance of any discussion of the social function of art becomes understandable when one realizes that it is the autonomy aesthetic [that] is the focal point of their analysis. The autonomy aesthetic . . . contains a definition of the function of art: it is conceived as a social realm that is set apart from the means-end rationality of daily bourgeois existence" (*The Theory of the Avant-Garde*, trans. Michael Shaw [Minneapolis: University of Minnesota Press, 1984], 10).

11. See Jochen Schulte-Sasse's introduction to Peter Bürger's *Theory of the Avant-Garde* for a more detailed description of this historical phenomenon. Bürger himself takes this idea a little further by saying that "the apartness from the praxis of life that had always constituted the institutional status of art in bourgeois society now becomes the content of works" (27).

12. This emphasis on the formal by the modernist poets evokes Jacques Derrida's theory of the *parergonal*, as I argue in the introduction of this book. "The *parergon*," Derrida says, "can augment the pleasure of taste, contribute to the proper and intrinsically aesthetic representation if it intervenes by its *form* and only by its form" (64). Form, then, enhances the esthetic pleasure of the viewer of a work because by framing the work (the text), it becomes a part of the work (the text).

13. See Charles Altieri and Wendy Steiner for discussions of representation and iconicity in abstract art. Wendy Steiner, *The Colors of Rhetoric: Problems in the Relation between Modern Literature and Painting* (Chicago: University of Chicago Press, 1982). They both believe that it is possible for art to lose iconicity.

14. As Steiner says, "The image and the diagram are relevant not only to the question of how poems can be like paintings, but also to how either complex sign can be like the reality it depicts" (*Colors of Rhetoric*, 20). For more detailed definitions of iconicity, see Steiner's *Colors of Rhetoric*, 2, 20, and 93; and Mitchell, 2, 56, and 60.

15. Altieri, 265.

16. Heuving, 51.

17. Theodor W. Adorno, *Aesthetic Theory*, ed. Gretel Adorno and Rolf Tiedemann, trans. C. Lenhardt (London: Routledge and Kegan Paul, 1986), 31.

18. Bürger reinforces this notion by saying that "the avant-gardiste protest, whose aim it is to reintegrate art into the praxis of life, reveals the nexus between autonomy and the absence of any consequences" (22).

19. The avant-gardists were not entirely estranged from the modernists by any means. In fact, Bürger argues that the avant-gardists directed "toward the practical the aesthetic experience (which rebels against the praxis of life) that Aestheticism developed" (34). Astradur Eysteinsson lays out very clearly the conflicting theories of the unity vs. the division of modernism and the avant-garde in *The Concept of Modernism* (Ithaca: Cornell University Press, 1990), 143–78.

20. Clifford Geertz, *The Interpretation of Culture* (New York: Basic Books, 1973), 448.

21. Ibid., 449.

22. Ibid., 7. I disagree with Geertz for two reasons, but I still think that his method provides a useful tool for the study of Moore's work. My criticisms of Geertz relate to Fraser's criticism of Lacan, and Kristeva by extension. By codifying cultural behavior into symbolic form, one always runs the risk of creating a system that is immutable and divorced from society. Both of these dangers are inherent in continental theory and allow

too-ready generalizations about a social order that comes to seem stratified and ossified, preventing analysis of heterogeneity and evolution. See Fraser, 188.

23. Jerome Bruner, *Acts of Meaning* (Cambridge: Harvard University Press, 1990), 20. Norman Bryson, in particular, sees the "production of meaning" in culture as "continuous": "it is mobility, volatility, the volatile encounter of the signifying practice with the political and economic practice surrounding it" (*Vision and Painting: The Logic of the Gaze* [New Haven: Yale University Press, 1983], 149).

24. Wilhelm Dilthey remarks that "meaning . . . arises in *memory*, in *cognition* of the *past*, and is concerned with negotiation about the 'fit' between past and present" (H. A. Hodge, *The Philosophy of Wilhelm Dilthey* [London, 1952], 272).

25. Hogue, 73.

26. Durham, 232.

27. DuPlessis, 71.

28. Miller, 9.

29. In his discussion of Wittgenstein, Henry Staten refers to the philosopher's "[involvement] in the kind of liberation of language as material substance from the domination of meaning which we associate with modern poetry: the concern with visual and auditory characteristics of words, with seemingly incidental connections of sound between words, with the use of metaphor as an irreducible mode of expression" (*Wittgenstein and Derrida* [Lincoln: University of Nebraska Press, 1984], 88). Michel Foucault's argument on the relation between power and discourse reinforces this type of thinking. See *The Order of Things: An Archaeology of the Human Sciences* (New York: Vintage, 1973).

30. Bryson identifies this power shift in *Vision and Painting: The Logic of the Gaze*. He says that "one is dealing not only with the transformative power of context and of the work of interpretation in context, but with the actual reversibility of power-relations: volatility is the keyword" (155).

31. This multivalent development in the arts corresponds to Foucault's theory of "double representations," which carry the meaning of a submerged or linked representation in addition to their own, by which they can create a new order (see esp. 221–44).

32. For more on Moore's relations to artists, see Costello, 186–214, and Leavell. For a more detailed description of Moore's relationship to Monroe Wheeler and of her connection through him to MOMA and its exhibits, see their correspondence at the Berg Collection, New York Public Library. Also, see Erickson and Hall for Moore's interaction with the Others group (Darlene Williams Erickson, *Illusion Is More Precise than Precision: The Poetry of Marianne Moore* [Tuscaloosa: University of Alabama Press, 1992]).

33. Bryson discusses the relationship between the work of art and its social context. He feels very strongly that the "image must be understood . . . as the milieu of the articulation of the reality known by a given visual community" (13), and later he supports this charge by saying that the arts "act as a supremely sensitive index of change within the social formation: painting, and, I would hold, poetry, must filter social change through the elaborate density of its technical practices" (16).

34. Along with Joanne Feit Deihl, I ascribe not timidity but rebellion to Moore's camouflage techniques. Diehl argues that the "marginalized poetic self exaggerates the style of the dominant culture," however, and that Moore shapes "her own version of poetic modernism without violating the contours of her familial and social identity" (*Women Poets and the American Sublime*. [Bloomington: Indiana University, 1990], 45,

and 60). I think that Moore does not hold back this far and that she does, indeed, resist those very codes of her personal and cultural identity.

35. This is the type of argument that can find no support in archival research, for Moore, even if she acknowledged this social transgression to herself, would never have acknowledged it in the public spheres of letters and lectures, or even the private one of her personal notebooks.

36. I take this synonym to be most accurate with respect to Moore, given her attitude toward the tremendously enlarged egos that she dismisses in "Novices," as I will discuss later.

37. The "incidental quality that occurs / as a concomitant of something well said" comes up in "The Past is the Present" when Moore recalls the words of her bible instructor: "'Hebrew poetry is prose / with a sort of heightened consciousness.'"

38. Julia Kristeva, *Revolution in Poetic Language*, trans. Margaret Waller (New York: Columbia University Press, 1984), 233.

39. Moore's amusement relates, I believe, to Kristeva's opinion that true ethical art pulverizes social "truths" "to the point of laughter" (233).

40. Adorno certainly believes that art needs continued adherence to its engendering milieu, but he contends that content represents the adherence to tradition, to historical immanence, and that form is the method by which the artists negate that engendering culture. See esp. 320–21.

41. See my discussion of Moore and dada for more on this topic.

42. This situation also relates to Foucault's history of representation and language in *The Order of Things*. Language, Foucault feels, lies between the idea and the object, representing this relationship while also analyzing it. Knowledge in the postclassical era has split, also according to the patterns of Moore's poetry, into the transcendental and the empirical.

43. Heuving, 156.

44. Schulze, *Web of Friendship,* 80.

45. For other discussions of "Roses Only," see Martin and Erickson.

46. Heuving, 80.

47. Hogue, 84.

48. See Martin and Erickson for readings of Williams's "The rose is obsolete" in comparison to Moore's "Roses Only."

49. Stanley Coffman says that Moore "chooses to write about an object . . . because she finds in it certain characteristics whose significance extends beyond the object" (*Imagism: A Chapter of the History of Modern Poetry* [Norman, OK: University of Oklahoma Press, 1951], 223).

50. DuPlessis connects these poems in her discussion of Moore's "Roses Only" by saying that H. D. "recasts the convention of roses in poetry. . . . This rose is not an iconic object of erotic veneration; instead it is resistant, hardened, harshly treated, but free" (86).

51. DuPlessis confirms this argument by saying that "the poem argues that the rose's intelligence exists and is an emanation of its beauty, yet that it is not its sexual availability and beauty that distinguish it, but rather its resistance to the tropes and the assumptions that would place it in the lyric tradition of unsurpassed and peerless gorgeousness" (85).

52. Chave also makes this connection between the objectification of the woman and her transformation into the phallus when she says: "To construct the female figure as a phallus is, in Freudian terms, a fetishistic strategy, a gesture at once of recognition and disavowal of the alarming fact that women have no penises" (605). Instead, I would hold that by turning a woman, or an image of a woman, into a phallus, she represents the power of the male who is viewing her—she has no power of her own. Hogue, too, relates the rose to the phallus in her reading of this poem (84).

53. Moore's vagueness in this poem deserves particular notice. She uses unassertive description in her retreat from confrontation: "delightful happen-so," "without-which-nothing," "what-is-this."

54. Heuving, 27.

55. See Costello: "Unlike the imagists, for whom the natural object was the adequate symbol, Moore drew objects into a realm of fancy where they could stand conspicuously for ideas" (*Imagining Possessions*, 38).

56. The very relegation of "Poetry" to the "Notes" section of Moore's *Complete Poems* indicates to me her endeavor to conceal the poem's truly subversive character. Heuving reinforces this sense of Moore's retreat from her original stance in this poem by calling our attention to the fact that Moore places herself in the position of audience here rather than of poet, as I indicated earlier "a position that enables her to establish her stance 'elsewhere'" and that allows her to avoid direct or obvious confrontation with her subject, her own culture (91).

57. In *Iconology: Image, Text, Ideology*, Mitchell emphasizes this role of the imagination by saying, "Perhaps the redemption of the imagination lies in accepting the fact that we create much of our world out of the dialogue between verbal and pictorial representations, and that our task is not to renounce this dialogue in favor of a direct assault on nature but to see that nature already informs both sides of the conversation" (46). Holley relates the pictorial and verbal in this poem also by saying that it is a "metaphor for the spatial imagination" (63).

58. Notable exceptions to this are present in the transcendental character of "When I Buy Pictures" and "The Plumet Basilisk" and in the sublimity of "An Octopus."

59. In this sense Moore is more radically modern than a poet such as Wallace Stevens because she breaks absolutely with romanticism.

60. William Butler Yeats, *Ideas of Good and Evil* (New York: Russell and Russell, 1967), 182.

61. Again, Moore's work outlines much of Foucault's theory of language and representation, that split between the transcendental and the empirical.

62. For other discussions of Moore's use of the imagination, see Martin, Stapleton, and Diehl (Laurence Stapleton, *Marianne Moore: The Poet's Advance* [Princeton: Princeton University Press, 1978]).

63. Heuving describes "To Statecraft Embalmed" and "To the Soul of Progress" as "poems of blame" (70).

64. This poem has drawn the attention of several critics, most notably Erickson (60–68) and DuPlessis (90). DuPlessis characterizes this poem as a satire, as "Roses Only" is a parody of courtly love poems. Further work needs to be done on the satirical and parodical aspects of Moore's work. Too often, it seems, critics take her at face value.

65. Buchloh identifies this promotion of the "esoteric elite" (i.e., that only real artists know how to make art and know how to make art that has correct goals) with the decay in

the artist's interest in addressing social issues ("Figures," 46). I do not think that this is the case with Moore's poetry, mostly because she sincerely would like to redress social and political problems. This poem does, however, remove her slightly from the mainstream avant-garde (if one does exist).

66. Moore uses a similar dissection metaphor as she proposes with the first line of this poem—"anatomize"—in "Those Various Scalpels," but in that poem, dissection is a benefit. Instead of dissecting themselves, as in this poem, the artists of that poem dissect society. See my discussion in the cubism chapter.

67. Erickson, 66.

68. This poem is particularly risky since Moore needs to show here what good poetry is.

69. Erickson compares this poem with precisionism and cubism (62). The wild activity here, however, is too mobilized. This poem could approach the dance of a Kandinsky but seems more appropriately an example of vorticism.

70. Heuving, 39.

71. Kristeva, 208.

72. Ibid., 60. See also Carolyn Burke's essential essay on modernist poetics and gender.

Chapter 2. "Prismatic Color": Marianne Moore's Cubism

1. See Wendy Steiner on Stein, particularly her discussion of cubism in "Literary Cubism: The Limits of the Analogy," in *Exact Resemblance,* 131–60.

2. Alfred H. Barr Jr., *Cubism and Abstract Art* (Cambridge: Belknap Press of Harvard University Press, 1986), 54.

3. Steiner, *Colors of Rhetoric*, 48.

4. Leo Steinberg, "The Philosophical Brothel," *October* 44 (spring 1988): 3–74.

5. Michael Fried, *Realism, Writing, Disfiguration* (Chicago: University of Chicago Press, 1987), 81.

6. Edward F. Fry, ed., *Cubism* (New York: McGraw-Hill, 1966), 297.

7. Nelson Goodman, *Languages of Art* (New York: Bobbs-Merrill, 1968), 230.

8. Ibid., 31.

9. Kendall Walton, *Mimesis as Makebelieve: On the Foundations of the Representational Arts* (Cambridge: Harvard University Press, 1990), 122.

10. See in particular my reading of "Camellia Sabina" and "The Jerboa" in the dada chapter.

11. Some contemporary critics, like Walter Pach, felt that the addition of abstraction to the arts through the cubist movement added more flexibility to the artist's resources: "The possibilities of expression were definitely increased with the change from the representation of the actual to the use of the abstract" (Walter Pach, "The Cubist Room," in vol. 2, *Pamphlets*, of *The Armory Show: International Exhibition of Modern Art, 1913* [New York: Arno Press, 1972], 54). Here, again, was the sense that art had used up all possible inspirations from nature and needed the new wealth created by the artist's interior as a producer of abstraction to give it a fresh subject. Pach, too, relies on the distinc-

tion between representation of nature and representation that bases itself on new notions of iconicity, those that engendered the abstraction of the arts of the twentieth century.

Charles Brinton, another early critic, also revised the role of nature in representation. He felt that cubist artists had withdrawn entirely from nature as the primary inspiration of the arts. Brinton wrote that in Picasso's work "sublime elementalism herewith gives place to divine geometrizing, with the result that we are at last free from all taint of nature imitation and watch unfold before us a world of visual imagery existing of and for itself alone" (Charles Brinton, "Evolution not Revolution in Art," *International Studio* 49 [April 1913]: 32). Brinton was aware of the removal of the artist from the external scene of nature into the cloistered environment of the studio. The cubist artist made his work in his mind, from interior inspiration, rather than from the exterior motivations of the natural world. Nature still played a part in the formulation of the work, but it was at a distance from the primary force of the intellect and imagination of the artist, making this art style increasingly abstract.

12. Fry, 300.

13. Steiner notes, in *Colors of Rhetoric,* that "the work of art [in cubism] signifies not reality, but the process of perceiving and conceiving of it" (181). See also Altieri, 265.

14. John Goulding, *Cubism: A History and an Analysis, 1907–1914* (London: Faber and Faber, 1988), xv.

15. For the complete history of the Armory Show, see Milton W. Brown, *The Story of the Armory Show* (New York: Abbeville Press and the Joseph Hirshhorn Foundation, 1988). For information about Stieglitz's loan of the Picasso drawing, see p. 97.

16. Christine Poggi says that "splintered and loosened from a verbal context, the words and letters in Cubist paintings and collages exemplify the same multivalence as the fragmentary pictorial forms, and in the variety of their typography take on a visual character in their own right" (*In Defiance of Painting: Cubism, Futurism and the Invention of Collage* [New Haven: Yale University Press, 1992], 28).

17. As I note earlier, in my discussion of Edward Fry's aesthetic theory, we make every effort, in the face of antinarratal material, to create the figure, the pattern to which we are accustomed.

18. In discussing Picasso's collages, Poggi points out that "insofar as a work of art is conceived as representational, it depends on the prior existence of a system of signs. Repetition is therefore a constituent factor in visual representation, just as it is in more obviously coded systems such as writing" (254).

19. Goulding, 74.

20. Ibid., 90.

21. Bram Dijkstra, *Cubism, Stieglitz, and the Early Poetry of William Carlos Williams: The Hieroglyphics of a New Speech* (Princeton: Princeton University Press, 1969), 66.

22. Ibid., 68.

23. Poggi concurs by saying that "chiaroscuro is divorced from its traditional function of modeling; fragmented bits of light and dark are dispersed throughout these canvases without regard for a consistent source of illumination," and later, "form is rendered in terms of rhythmically alternating light and dark planes, which do not correspond to a consistent source of light" (32 and 46).

24. Marius DeZayas, "Pablo Picasso," *Camera Work* 34–35 (April–July 1911): 67.

25. Poggi theorizes that this "divorce of color from form" is a "way of preserving it from the distortions of chiaroscuro and of returning to an ideal of pure local color. . . . Color should be regarded as an attribute of material substance rather than as a changeable effect of light" (13–14).

26. Here again, as I noted in my earlier discussion of the graphic in cubism, we are most immediately drawn in an abstract painting to what we can most easily recognize. The graphic continues to bear its adherence to the bourgeois culture, but it also serves to reject that culture by its new context in the sharply abstract world of the cubist.

27. Miller stresses Moore's cubist technique by saying that her "use of negation, of antithesis, of contradiction in almost every aspect of her poetic structure resembles Bohr's concept of complementarity: phenomena are known most clearly by being seen from multiple and paradoxical points of observation. Moore's familiarity with cubism's presentation of multiple perspectives simultaneously would only have strengthened her attraction to such principles" (47).

28. Marianne Moore, *The Complete Prose*, ed. Patricia Willis (New York: Viking, 1987), 506.

29. Barr, 77–79.

30. DeZayas, 67.

31. Clement Greenberg, "Collage," in *Collage: Critical Views*, ed. Katherine Hoffman (Ann Arbor: UMI Research Press, 1989), 68.

32. Another way to see Moore's cubist refraction technique is through the analogy that Costello uses: the prism (205–6).

33. See Erickson for a complete discussion of "The Fish" (129–35). She also uses the metaphor of the kaleidoscope, while Kenner speaks of it in terms of the mosaic (Hugh Kenner, *A Homemade World: The American Modernist Writers* [New York: Alfred A. Knopf, 1975]). Most critics address this poem, including Heuving, Miller, Durham, and Holley.

34. *The Egoist* 5 (August 1918): 83.

35. Durham does a lovely reading of the sexual underpinnings of this poem (226).

36. Heuving notes this ambiguity of referent, arguing that it "intensifies the sense that powers inhere in things rather than in motions, in objects rather than in their symbolic meanings" (97). Given what I argue in my first chapter, however, I feel that Moore's main investment in her poetry is in what she calls "value" and "principle," concepts that adhere suprameanings to these objects and animals.

37. To Holley, "the poem is the water," emphasizing the cubist nonhierarchical placement of objects side by side, rather than foreground moving into background (62).

38. Kirk Varnedoe, *A Fine Disregard* (New York: Museum of Modern Art, 1990), 180. Fragmentation is the type of technique that Moore relies on in her "The Fish," as discussed earlier.

39. Gertrude Stein, "Picasso," *Camera Work* special number (August 1912): 29–30.

40. Steiner, *Exact Resemblance*, 152.

41. Ibid., 154.

42. Steiner suggests that "whereas literature normally develops its subjects gradually from one sentence to the next, supplying new information as it proceeds, Stein's subjects were to be totally present, fully developed, in each atemporal sentence" (*Exact Resem-*

blance, 145). I think, instead, that Stein was trying to condense disparate terms, to compress time rather than displaying a full hand of cards every minute or so.

43. DuPlessis, 95. Erickson and Leavell relate "Those Various Scalpels" to cubism but in terms of "the reduction of figures to basic forms and the creation of austere monochromatic figures" (Leavell, 53). Who this poem portrays is open to speculation. I see this poem as the depiction of a Renaissance figurine of a woman, but I have been unable to verify it through consultations with experts in Renaissance art history. Erickson sees this figure as the representation of a modern woman; Heuving lists other possibilities, such as "a twentieth-century femme fatale," a "woman warrior," a "symbol of the patriarchal state," "a seventeenth-century knight or soldier" (175); Burke cites evidence that the poem may be about Mina Loy (112). DuPlessis refers to this portrait as another gender challenging genre, like the romantic love lyric of "Novices" and carpe diem of "Roses Only" (85, 90, and 95 n. 32).

44. The sounds of the scalpels make more sense as the poem progresses and as we realize the sounds are produced by the clutch of "lances" in the figure's hand, yet the illogic of the moment at the beginning of the poem takes precedence here.

45. While we do not yet know to whom Moore is speaking, the poem finally allows us to pull the pieces of these parts of the image together in the same way that we pull together Picasso's drawing to see a nude woman, so that we can determine by the end of the poem that Moore refers to a statue of some kind. Just as Steinberg says that we use our stored memories of images to reconstruct cubist fragments into a recognizable image, we compile the pieces of this figurine into its whole through our recognition and reconstruction of its fragments.

46. Signature has quite a number of definitions, all of which could come into play in this situation: a person's name, or a mark representing it; any unique distinguishing aspect, feature, or mark; a mark placed on the first page of every sheet to guide the binder in folding and gathering them; serving to identify or distinguish a person, group, etc. All of these are interesting in conjunction with Moore's adjective, "ambiguous," because each sense of signature indicates a specific identity, while ambiguous denies that very certainty.

Chapter 3. "Anthology of Words": Marianne Moore's Collage

1. The fuller version of this article appeared as Theodore Roosevelt, "A Layman's Views of an Art Exhibition," *Outlook* 103 (29 March 1913): 718–20. This section is probably either from *The Literary Digest* or *Current Opinion* because these were Moore's two sources for her Armory Show articles. This excerpt from Roosevelt's article was entitled "Mr. Roosevelt and the Cubists."

2. Ibid., 719.

3. Ibid.

4. *Current Opinion* 54.4 (April 1913): 310–11.

5. Monroe Wheeler, Moore's contemporary and a curator at the Museum of Modern Art, was one of the first to identify Moore as a collage poet (Monroe Wheeler, "Reminiscence," in *Festschrift for Marianne Moore's Seventy-seventh Birthday by Various Hands* [New York: Tambimuttu and Mass, 1964], 127–30). Costello also has a lengthy discussion of Moore's collage techniques.

6. Henry Staten identifies the same transference operating in Wittgenstein's theoretical writings: "Philosophy . . . is like a form of poetry or collage, word-collage, language treated from outside as preexistent material with which constructions having a certain configuration can be devised" (86).

7. See William Rubin's "Picasso and Braque: An Introduction" for a more thorough description of the implications of this first collage (in *Picasso and Braque: Pioneering Cubism* [New York: Museum of Modern Art, 1989], 36–38).

8. Christine Poggi relates collage to "the decisive moment of rupture with the past, when the autonomy of painting gave way to a vast array of new signifying practices" (257).

9. Patricia Leighton, "'La Propagande par le Rire': Satire's Subversion in Apollinaire, Jarry and Picasso's Collages," *Gazette de Beaux Arts* 12 (October 1988): 167.

10. Marc Dachy, *Dada: The Dada Movement, 1915–1923* (New York: Rizzoli, 1990), 8.

11. Marjorie Perloff, "The Invention of Collage," in *Collage*, ed. Jeannine Parisier Plottel (New York: New York Literary Forum, 1983), 10.

12. Marcel Duchamp, *Dadas on Art*, ed. Lucy R. Lippard (Englewood Cliffs, N.J.: Prentice-Hall, 1971), 141.

13. Jacob Korg, "The Dialogic Nature of Collage in Pound's *Cantos*," *Mosaic* 22.2 (spring 1989): 96.

14. Ibid., 96.

15. Leavell argues that there is a difference between the type of quotation used by Pound and Eliot and that used by Williams and Moore: "Moore's extensive use of quotations and especially the dailiness of their sources—newspapers, advertisements—have made her affinities with collage seem obvious. . . . Whereas the quotations in Pound and Eliot are primarily from privileged texts of literature, history, and religion, the sources of quotation in Moore and Williams (especially in *Paterson*) are more democratic, more transient, more random" (102). Lisa M. Steinman also sees this style of quotation selection as "democratizing," but she also sees it as a "redefinition of culture itself," in accordance with my argument that the artist seeks cultural change in those aspects particularly confining or restrictive (108).

16. Several studies on Moore's use of quotations have recently been published, including Erickson's third chapter and Elizabeth Gregory's chapter on Moore ("Marianne Moore's Poetry of Quotation," in *Quotation and Modern American Poetry: "Imaginary Gardens with Real Toads"* [Houston: Rice University Press, 1996], 129–85). See, in particular, new discussions of "Marriage," including: Erickson, 93–113; Miller, 178–79; Hogue, 95–100; Heuving, 121–31; Holley 66–68; and Diehl 61–70. Also see further criticism on Moore's "editing" of quotations: Hogue, 78–79; and Heuving, 128. Leavell argues that Moore changed her quotations as a method of "self-protection" (114).

17. Diehl, too, views "Marriage" as subversive (61).

18. Gilbert argues that "Marriage" depicts "Moore's feminist inclination to deconstruct patriarchal history from the perspective of a nonparticipant in crucial sexual institutions even while it allowed her to reconstruct a history of her own—a *natural* history in which she and her familiar familial animals played a central part" as in "An Octopus" (38).

19. Quoted in Schulman, 159. Miller contends that "while appearing to belittle herself, [Moore] instead shifts the terms of value by which one judges worth hearing, what

empowers readers and previous speakers as well as what empowers herself" (5).

20. Rosenbach Museum and Library, 1251/7. This stenographer's notebook is a treasure trove of Moore's poetic process.

21. As Patricia Willis has noted, these early versions of "Marriage" are often conjoined with those of "An Octopus," as if Moore first thought of the two poems as one (Patricia Willis, "The Road to Paradise: First Notes on 'An Octopus.'" *Twentieth Century Literature* 30 [summer/fall 1984]: 247).

22. Rosenbach Museum and Library, 1251/7: 4, 15, 22, 26; 5, 13, 22; 13; 18; 23.

23. Keller confirms this by noting that Moore uses quotations from known sources to "release her from conventional feminine docility and decorum, enabling her to criticize the institution that many regard as women's sole purpose, without discrediting herself" (Lynn Keller, "'For inferior who is free?' Liberating the Woman Writer in Marianne Moore's 'Marriage'" in *Influence and Intertextuality in Literary History*, ed. Jay Clayton and Eric Rothstein [Madison: University of Wisconsin Press, 1991], 228).

24. Willis, 252.

25. Holley found this quotation in the Rosenbach Museum and Library 1250/4, 29–30.

26. Pamela White Hadas confirms this notion by saying that "Moore's quotation of Bacon, so aptly placed for rendering the symbol of love into an image of social greed, and the eternal circle into an image of unprogressive self-interest, applies as much to a style of writing and speaking as it does to the life style of prospective husbands and wives" (Pamela White Hadas, *Marianne Moore: Poet of Affection* [Syracuse, N.Y.: Syracuse University Press, 1977], 143).

27. Philip Littell, Review of George Santayana's poetry, *The New Republic* 34.433 (21 March 1923): 102.

28. Littell includes in this review the quotation, "Les choses valent toujours mieux dans leur source," a belief that Moore is trying to contradict in her collage method.

29. William Hazlitt, "On the Prose Style of Poets," in *The Complete Works of William Hazlitt*, ed. P. P. Howe (London: Dent, 1930–34), 12:10.

30. Edward Thomas, *Feminine Influence on the Poets* (London: Martin Secker, 1910).

31. Ibid., 111.

32. William Godwin, *Enquiry Concerning Political Justice and Its Influence on Morals and Happiness*, ed. F. E. L. Priestley (Toronto: University of Toronto Press, 1946), 507.

33. Anthony Trollope, *Barchester Towers* (New York: Dodd, Mead, 1904), 2:147.

34. William Shakespeare, *The Tempest* 2.2.182.

35. Abraham Mitram Rihbany, *The Syrian Christ* (Boston: Houghton Mifflin, 1916), 272.

36. Ibid., 333.

37. Lynn Keller and Christanne Miller, "'The Tooth of Disputation': Marianne Moore's 'Marriage,'" *Sagetrieb* 6.3 (winter 1987): 99–116; Stephen Bann, "Collage: The Poetics of Discontinuity?" *Word and Image* 4.1 (1988): 353.

38. Charles Reade, *Christie Johnstone* [1885] (Paris: The Grolier Society, n.d.), 14.

39. I have been unable to track down a specific source for this quotation, but this sentiment can be found in numerous speeches and articles by Edmund Burke, such as

those found on pages 398–99 and 406–7 in Peter J. Stanlis, ed., *Edmund Burke: Selected Writings and Speeches* (Gloucester, Mass.: Peter Smith, 1968).

40. My thanks go to Cynthia Hogue for this suggestion (private communication).

41. Holley, 104.

42. James Clifford, *The Predicament of Culture* (Cambridge: Harvard University Press, 1988), 121. Mitchell suggests the same act of "defamiliarization" as Clifford, but with more force when textual and "imagistic elements" interact: "A familiar practice which might be 'defamiliarized' by understanding it as a transgression, an act of (sometimes ritual) violence involving an incorporation of the symbolic Other into the generic Self" (157).

43. Diehl also sees "Marriage and "An Octopus" as companion poems (71). For a most thorough description of Moore's composition of "An Octopus," see Willis. Costello mentions that "the pamphlet of *National Parks Rules and Regulations* includes an aerial photograph of Mt. Rainier that makes it look like an octopus, and the prose caption calls it an 'octopus of ice'" (259 n. 17). The Rosenbach Museum and Library has Moore's copy of this pamphlet with her marginalia. Costello also says in this book on Moore that the "octopus is a metaphor for the glacier, but in a later article she comes closer to my reading of the poem when she says that "Pound and H. D. join Moore in using the octopus as an image of the mind" ("Marianne Moore and the Sublime," 9).

44. See John Meyer Slatin for this kind of reading (*"The Savage's Romance": The Poetry of Marianne Moore* [University Park: Pennsylvania State University Press, 1986], 156–57).

45. For these readings, see Costello, Willis and Molesworth. Slatin argues that the poem represents the poet's passage from an inability to name things, especially those in nature, as represented by the cubist breakup and refraction of images, to a reconstruction of identity (174).

46. Here again, see Willis, 257–64, on the influence of the Greeks on Moore. Apparently Moore was reading Newman (*Historical Sketches*) and William de Witt Hyde (*The Five Great Philosophies of Life*). Holley describes Moore's lengthy cataloguing in this poem as one that "increase[s] opacity and object-ivity" rather than the greater clarity that a catalogue would normally produce (65).

47. For more details on these trips of Moore's, see Molesworth's biography of Moore and Willis's essay.

48. Slatin says that "one of [the] functions [of quotation] is to serve . . . as 'lenses'—or lenses within lenses . . . by which vision is, if only slightly, distorted" (174).

49. While less concerned with Moore's subversive intention, Diehl also notes the sublimity of "An Octopus," as does Schulze (*Web of Friendship,* 51–62).

50. *The National Parks Portfolio*, Department of the Interior Rules and Regulations, 1922. Rosenbach Museum and Library.

51. Clifton Johnson, *What to See in America* (New York: Macmillan, 1919), 410. This quotation appears in one of Moore's poetry notebooks at the Rosenbach Museum and Library, 1251/7, 79. The quotation here comes directly from Moore's notebook. Johnson's actual words are: "[The winds] cut the bark from the windward side of the trees, and shear off the tender twigs that have started in exposed places during the previous summer. The prevailing westerly wind bends the trees so that many have the appearance of trying to escape. In some places the trees develop only where they are afforded special protection, such as the leeward side of a bowlder [sic]. In this struggle with wind

and flying sand, cold, and nine months of snow they seldom attain a height of over eight feet, and many grow along the ground like vines" (411).

52. W. D. Wilcox, *The Rockies of Canada* (New York: Putnam, 1903), 13–14.

53. Johnson, 514.

54. Rosenbach Museum and Library 1251/7 80; Johnson, 537. Johnson's word is actually "bustling" rather than "bristling." In this case Moore has added a note of angry hairy quality as opposed to Johnson's view of these men as merely industrious.

55. See both Willis (244–45) and Molesworth (105) on these names. Molesworth also notes that the very close friend of Moore's family, Mary Norcross, who influenced Moore in deciding to go to college at Bryn Mawr, Norcross's own alma mater, is called "Beaver" by the Moore family (Molesworth, 31).

56. *The National Parks Portfolio*, 28.

57. Wilcox, 66.

58. *The National Parks Portfolio*, 28. All underlinings are Moore's.

59. Ibid., 9.

60. Francis Ward, "'Poison-Gas' in Nature: The Lesser Octopus," *Illustrated London News* 163 (11 August 1923), p. 270.

61. Slatin too says that "indeed the poem *does* describe 'a circle': like the road, 'it ends' 'where snow begins'" (160).

62. Costello strengthens the connections between "An Octopus" and cubism when she says, "The glacier . . . demands rapid eye movement to keep up with the rush of detail" (*Imaginary Possessions*, 94).

Chapter 4. Dada Subversion: Hannah Höch and Marianne Moore

1. Even so, I must disagree with such critics as Erickson, who contends outright that Moore's work has no relation to dada (67).

2. Moore's moral stance surfaces in her poetry most typically in the form of aphorisms. Periodically, she will arrest the movement of a poem by presenting a clear statement of criticism or admonishment, as I will show in "The Jerboa" and "Camellia Sabina." Even so, her emphasis on "value" and "principle," as I have argued in my discussion of "To a Snail," indicates the importance to her of morality in the special sense of culturally critical.

3. Moore uses these images as if they were found objects, items found randomly and appropriated for her own poems. This is an extension of Kenner's view of quotations as found objects.

4. The origin of the title of the movement, for instance, is under debate, depending on the source consulted. According to Richard Huelsenbeck, it was a randomly chosen word out of a French/German dictionary; "dada" in French is a child's word for a rocking horse but also a word for a hobby or obsession. Hans Richter recalled "dada" as from the Romanian speech of Tristan Tzara and Marcel Janco: "Yes, yes," "Da, da." See H. Harvard Arnason, *History of Modern Art: Painting, Sculpture, Architecture, Photography,*

3rd ed. (New York: Abrams, 1986), 291; Francis M. Naumann, *New York Dada, 1915–1923* (New York: Abrams, 1994), 10.

5. Arnason, 306.

6. Ibid.

7. Benjamin Buchloh quotes George Grosz's words by saying that montage let the dadaists "speak publicly with hidden meaning" ("Allegorical Procedures: Appropriation and Montage in Contemporary Art," *Artforum* 21.1 [September 1982]: 43). Berlin dadaists, according to Buchloh, could say in photomontage "what would have been banned by the censors if we had said it in words" (43). Maud Lavin discusses this aspect of photomontage, also, in *Cut with the Kitchen Knife: The Weimar Photomontages of Hannah Höch* (New Haven: Yale University Press, 1993), 23–29.

8. Annabelle Melzer, *Dada and Surrealist Performance* (Baltimore: The Johns Hopkins University Press, 1994), 30–44.

9. See Henri Behar and Michel Carassou's *Dada: Histoire d'une subversion* for a discussion of dada's focus on the destruction of society in order to rebuild it. Dada becomes, then, a moral movement, one that decries the complacency and blind acceptance of the bourgeoisie (*Dada: Histoire d'une subversion* [Paris: Fayard, 1990], 30). John E. Bowlt agrees by saying, "These exaggerated gestures were stimulated by the urge to create rather than destroy, to affirm a new code rather than to destroy all norms" ("Dada in Russia," in *Dada/Dimensions*, ed. Stephen Foster [Ann Arbor: UMI Research Press, 1985], 224).

10. "Fotomontage" in *A-Z* 16 (May 1931). Reprinted in *Raoul Hausmann*, exhibition catalogue (Hannover: Kestnergesellschaft, 1981), 51, and in Benjamin H. D. Buchloh, "Allegorical Procedures: Appropriation and Montage in Contemporary Art," *Artforum* 21.1 (September 1982): 43.

11. Behar and Carassou agree that "Dada was not merely a reaction against the war," but they feel that dada was not trying to operate on the level of the culture as a whole but rather on that of language. Dada is a "demolition enterprise which attacked first the edifice of language" (26, translation my own).

12. Tristan Tzara, "Lecture on Dada," in *Seven Dada Manifestos and Lampisteries*, trans. Barbara Wright (New York: Riverrun Press, 1977), 110. Because of its fiercely political stance, dada produced a great number of manifestos, each of a similar nature. Jean Arp, for instance, wrote, "Dada is the basis of all art. Dada is for the senseless which doesn't mean nonsense. Dada is as senseless as nature. Dada is for nature and against 'art.' Dada is direct like nature and tries to assign each thing to its essential place" (quoted in Jane Hancock, "Arp's Chance Collages," in *Dada/Dimensions*, ed. Stephen C. Foster [Ann Arbor: UMI Research Press, 1985], 64).

13. For more on relations between dada and technology, see Hanne Bergius, "The Ambiguous Aesthetic of Dada: Towards a Definition of its Categories," in *Dada: Studies of a Movement*, ed. Richard Sheppard (Norfolk: Alpha Academic, 1979), 36; "dada machinel," in *Kunst und Technik in den 20er Jahren: Neue Sachlichkeit und Gegenständlicher Konstructivismus* 2 July-10 August 1980 (München: Städtische Galerie im Lenbachhaus); and Tim Mathews, "The Machine: Dada Vorticism and the Future," in *The Violent Muse: Violence and the Artistic Imagination in Europe, 1910–1939*, ed. Jana Howlett and Rod Mengham (Manchester: Manchester University Press, 1994), 124–40.

14. Edouard Roditi, "Interview with Hannah Höch," *Arts* 34.3 (December 1959): 26.

15. Gertrud Jula Dech, *Schnitt mit dem Küchenmesser DADA durch die letzte weimarer Bierbauchkulturepoche Deutschlands: Untersuchungen zur Fotomontage bei*

Hannah Höch (Munster: Lit. Verlag, 1981). Maud Lavin, *Cut with the Kitchen Knife: The Weimar Photomontages of Hannah Höch* (New Haven: Yale University Press, 1993).

16. Johanna Drucker describes Höch's method as that of "involved with investigating the intersection between the private imaginary and the production of identity as a social category" ("Dada Collage and Photomontage," *Art Journal* 52 [winter 1993]: 84).

17. The dadaists had a particular interest in producing work that was ephemeral and that would not be stable over time; this was another expression of their disgust with traditional artistic productions. Bergius notes that "by means of the destruction of illusion which is implicit in its form, the montage challenged conventional modes of perception and called into question the traditional consonance between the whole of a picture and its component parts" ("Ambiguous Aesthetic," 34). Höch's compositional weaknesses, then, would probably have been intentional.

18. Lavin devotes an extensive section to this photomontage and also relies on Dech for Höch's sources. Lavin, however, stresses the importance of women in this collage. They are certainly present, and since they are often represented as dancers (an important dada symbol for chaos), they are important. But in the larger context of the work, it is the male images that predominate. Lavin's argument is undermined, for instance, by her efforts to make Höch's treatment of Kathe Köllwitz seem flattering when Köllwitz appears in the center of the collage but decapitated (only her head is present) and with a stake through her head. See Lavin, 19–46.

19. Naumann notes that "recent evidence has demonstrated that a select group of artists in New York were aware of the dada movement in Europe shortly after the word first appeared in print. Moreover, it is now clear that by the time they first learned of the dada movement in Europe, a number of American artists had already embraced and employed the basic principles and ideologies that inspired their European colleagues" (10).

20. Lucy Lippard, ed. *Dadas on Art* (Englewood Cliffs, N.J.: Prentice-Hall, 1971), 140.

21. Estera Milman, "Dada New York: An Historiographic Analysis," in *Dada/Dimensions*, ed. Stephen Foster (Ann Arbor: UMI Research Press, 1985), 174.

22. See, for instance, Buchloh's "Allegorical Procedures." Much of Buchloh's argument is focused on Walter Benjamin's notion of the allegorical as a "[protest] against [the object's] devaluation to the status of a commodity" (44).

23. Green, 44 and 23.

24. Ibid., 38.

25. Kristeva, 83.

26. Leavell, 173. From Emmy Veronica Sanders, "America Invades Europe," *Broom* 1 (November 1921): 90–91.

27. Moore's interest in technology has not gone unnoticed by critics. See especially Daniel L. Guillory's "Marianne Moore and Technology," in *Marianne Moore: Woman and Poet*, ed. Patricia C. Willis (Orono: National Poetry Foundation, University of Maine, 1990), 83–91. Martin, too, relates modernism to the machine (xi-xii).

28. In proving that science increasingly became a model for avant-garde artists, Green quotes an interview of Duchamp: "I was interested in introducing the precise and exact aspect of science." Green goes on to say that if Duchamp "wanted science to subvert nineteenth-century art, he subverted science too" (39). This is exactly what Moore is trying to do—to use science to subvert traditional art, but to subvert science in order to subvert the bourgeoisie.

29. Martin describes Moore's poetic technique as "scientific method broken down by language" (117).

30. Other readings of "The Jerboa" appear in Schulze (*Web of Friendship*), Judith Merrin (*An Enabling Humility: Marianne Moore, Elizabeth Bishop, and the Uses of Tradition* [New Brunswick, N.J.: Rutgers University Press, 1990]), Heuving, and Miller, among others.

31. Gilbert, 41

32. Schulze, *Web of Friendship,* 88.

33. Gilbert, 40.

34. Miller, 148, and Heuving, 155, call attention to Moore's antihierarchical argument in this poem.

35. Moore drew the references to the cane and the portable bedroom from several issues of the *Illustrated London News*. An article by J. D. S. Pendlebury, "The 'Castle of the Disc' at Tell el Amarna," contains a photograph of "two ivory walking stick handles in the shape of hands" (*Illustrated London News,* 19 March 1932, p. 428). The palace belonged to the Pharaoh Akhenaten (1375–58 B.C.), the husband of Nefertiti.

The folding bedroom is pictured in an article by George A. Reisner: "The Golden Travelling Bed of the Mother of Cheops" (*Illustrated London News,* 19 March 1932, pp. 767–69).

36. Because the jerboa is of the rat family, and because "Rat" was Moore's nickname within her family, Schulze considers this poem to be a self-portrait (*Web of Friendship,* 83).

37. This is an interesting notion, given current sensitivity about colonialism. That an entire continent should be identified by the relationship of its northern shore to a conquering force long since dissipated is revealing. Moore's subtle critique of this situation reveals not only her close scrutiny of the jerboa but her sense of repudiation of the attitude that this name expresses. Underscoring this view is Moore's adaptation of the Latin definition for Africanus: "Of or connected with Africa, esp. the Roman province African." The entire continent is named after the Roman province, but it is Moore who stresses the notion of the Romans as conquerors, who established thereby the identity of the continent.

38. Miller, 129.

39. Ibid., 139.

40. Moore's reference to the jerboa's daytime activities are odd, considering her normal concern for accuracy. The jerboa is a strictly nocturnal animal that escapes the blistering heat of the desert by crawling into its burrow.

41. Merrin, 21, and Miller describe the jerboa as evincing the proper behavior in Moore's opinion. Miller sees it as a "moral exemplum," (148).

42. Schulze, *Web of Friendship,* 88, and Slatin, 206, note the resemblance of the poem's rhythm to the jerboa's movement.

43. For more on Moore and the machine, see Guillory. Note, too, poems such as "To a Steam Roller" and the uncollected "To the Soul of 'Progress'" (*The Egoist* 2.4 [1 April 1915]: 62).

44. Heuving, 155; Slatin, 207; Schulze, *Web of Friendship,* 90–91.

45. Schulze, *Web of Friendship,* 90.

46. Schulze also compares the similarities between the endings of these poems (*Web of Friendship*, 90–91).

47. "To Browning," *The Egoist* 2 (2 August 1915): 126.

48. Robert Browning, *The Ring and the Book* (New York: Norton, 1961), 1.32.

49. Ibid., 1.408. I am deriving much of my reading of Browning's poem from the essay on it by Wylie Sypher, who says that to Browning "the truth is composite" (viii).

50. Sypher, xiv.

51. Ibid., xvii.

52. *The Letters of Robert Browning and Elizabeth Barrett, 1945–1846* (New York: Harper, 1899), 1:513 and 2:38.

53. "Radical," *Others* 5 (March 1919): 15.

54. Note here, for example, the overwhelming interest in the gender of newborn babies. Gender is always the first question asked about the newborn, long before the name, and in these days of prenatal testing, questions of gender arise very early in pregnancy.

55. This blithe reference to circumstance, as if contingency played into where a carrot "lives," recalls the "happen-so" of "Roses Only."

56. Gilbert notes this sense of Moore as a cultural "outsider" because of her unmarried, childless state (35).

Afterword

1. In his 1924 "Manifesto of Surrealism," André Breton lists even more participants, including Roger Vitrac, Georges Auric, Jean Paulhan, Max Morise, Benjamin Péret, Joseph Delteil, Jean Carrive, George Limbour, Marcel Noll, T. Fraenkel, Georges Malkine, Antonin Artaud, Francis Gérard, Pierre Naville, J.-A. Boiffard, Jacques Baron, "and gorgeous women, [he] might add" (*Manifestos of Surrealism*, trans. Richard Seaver and Helen R. Lane [Ann Arbor: The University of Michigan Press, 1972], 17).

2. Marianne Moore, "Concerning the Marvelous" (Archives of American Art 2166, Column 523, Alfred Barr papers), 1. My thanks go to Dickran Tashjian for so thoughtfully presenting me with the gift of this essay by Moore. This shift in emphasis from the visual to the literary may be evidence of the "social and cultural upheaval" that John McCole argues was producing "a radically new humanity" (218). He calls this an "epochal shift in the modes of perception" (217). John McCole, *Walter Benjamin and the Antinomies of Tradition* (Ithaca: Cornell University Press, 1993).

3. Breton, 151.

4. Ibid., 26.

5. Ibid., 9.

6. Walter Benjamin, "Surrealism: The Last Snapshot of the European Intelligentsia," in *One Way Street and Other Writings*, trans. Edmund Jephcott and Kingsley Shorter (New York: Harcourt Brace, 1978), 226.

7. John McCole argues this point more extensively in his book on Walter Benjamin, where he says that estheticism "was both an attitude toward life and a doctrine about the function of art in bourgeois society—the idea that art serves no purpose and is not to be

subjected to the criteria of utility and morality by which social phenomena are normally judged" (208).

8. Benjamin, "Surrealism," 232–33. Benjamin, in fact, saw the surrealists as revolutionary Marxists, as is evident when he says, "Only when in technology body and image so interpenetrate that all revolutionary tension becomes bodily collective innervation, and all the bodily innervations of the collective become revolutionary discharge, has reality transcended itself to the extent demanded by the *Communist Manifesto*" (239).

9. McCole confirms this suggestion by arguing that "the surrealist movement was driven by both of these impulses—the aesthetes' radicalization of the autonomy of art and the avant-garde's rebellion against the social institutionalization of that very autonomy" (210). My term "radicalization" comes from McCole also (209).

10. Paul Ricoeur sees the goal of Freudian analysis as the "dispossession" of "consciousness . . . because the act of becoming conscious is its task" (439). Paul Ricoeur, *Freud and Philosophy: An Essay on Interpretation*, trans. Denis Savage (New Haven: Yale, 1970).

11. See the artwork of Salvador Dali, René Magritte, and Paul Delvaux for just a few examples of illustrations of dreams.

12. McCole, 232.

13. Moore, "Concerning the Marvelous," 4. Moore also lauds in this essay Max Ernst's ability to display on his canvas all the clarity possible, but a clarity that does nothing to answer all questions: "Max Ernst's voracity for a definiteness that cannot defeat mystery [is an effect] of lasting value for poetry" (2).

14. For a fuller explanation of the relations of dreams to history see McCole, 219–20.

15. Louis Aragon, *Paris Peasant*, trans. Simon Watson Taylor (Boston: Exact Change, 1980), 128.

16. Walter Benjamin, *Gesammelte Schriften*, ed. Rolf Tiedemann and Hermann Schweppenhäuser (Frankfurt: Suhrkamp, 1972–89), 5:1046. Translation for this quotation by McCole, 243.

17. Ibid., 1026–27.

18. Leavell, 124.

19. Note here the similarity between "New York" and "The Jerboa" in their complaint about materialism and the overly wealthy.

20. Miller, 72–73.

21. Heuving concurs with me here when she says, "Training her reader's consciousness away from the reifications and over-determinations of existing thought, Moore affirms the palpability of phenomena" (100).

22. Ibid., 104. The others in this series include "England," "When I Buy Pictures," "New York," and "The Labors of Hercules."

23. Slatin corroborates this sense of the past working through into the present in this poem. He writes: "The poem's implicit argument concerns the relationship between the present and the past—or, more precisely, what Moore by now perceives as the dangerous absence of any such relationship. This is not a nostalgic complaint that the present differs from the past and is therefore worse; the point is rather that the world of the present in [this poem is] a city of isolation and death which has no consciousness of the past at all—and that consciousness, as the poem's closing lines imply, *is* life" (129).

24. Heuving, 105.

25. Both Costello and Slatin identify the "dried bone" in the "arrangement" as a quotation from a letter written by William Carlos Williams to Marianne Moore: "I cannot object to rhetoric, as you point out, but I must object to the academic associations with which rhetoric is hung and which vitiate all its significance by making the piece of work to which it is applied a dried bone." This antiacademic attitude is equally prevalent in the surrealist enterprise as supporting a less logical and more random train of thought as a route to the unveiling of the unconscious. Slatin, 128; Costello, 161; Williams, *Selected Letters*, ed. John Thirwall (New York: McDowell, Oblensky, 1984), 52–53.

26. I include the units in Moore's list of what she dislikes because in the *Observations* version of this poem the second stanza ends with a colon. Note that in the *Complete Poems* this stanza ends with a comma, making her disapproval of the "bad furniture" that follows much more oblique. These units are remarkably like the array of small drawers and storage units that Joseph Cornell kept for sorting elements of his boxes. Dickran Tashjian argues convincingly that Moore was heavily influenced by this organizational style and by the tactic of composing disparate objects into the congruity of a single box, as evidenced by their extensive correspondence. See Dickran Tashjian, *Joseph Cornell: Gifts of Desire* (Miami Beach, Fla.: Grassfield, 1992).

27. Benjamin, "Surrealism," 237. McCole discusses the translation of the word that Benjamin uses in his essay on surrealism. The German word is "Rausch," which comes closer to ecstasy in meaning and does not necessarily refer to the effect of drugs or alcohol. McCole, 225 n.

28. Slatin, 134.

Select Bibliography

Adams, Adeline. "The Secret of Life." *Art and Progress* 4 (April 1913).

Adorno, Theodor W. *Aesthetic Theory*. Edited by Gretel Adorno and Rolf Tiedemann. Translated by C. Lenhardt. London: Routledge and Kegan Paul, 1986.

Altieri, Charles. *Painterly Abstraction in Modernist Poetry: The Contemporaneity of Modernism*. Cambridge: Cambridge University Press, 1989.

Aragon, Louis. *Paris Peasant*. Translated by Simon Watson Taylor. Boston: Exact Change, 1980.

Arnason, H. Harvard. *History of Modern Art: Painting, Sculpture, Architecture, Photography*. 3rd ed. New York: Abrams, 1986.

Bakhtin, Mikhail M. *The Dialogic Imagination*. Edited by Michael Holquist. Translated by Caryl Emerson and Michael Holquist. Austin: University of Texas Press, 1981.

Bann, Stephen. "Collage: The Poetics of Discontinuity?" *Word and Image* 4.1 (1988): 353–63.

Barr, Alfred H. Jr. *Cubism and Abstract Art*. Cambridge: Belknap Press of Harvard University Press, 1986.

Behar, Henri, and Michel Carassou. *Dada: Histoire d'une subversion*. Paris: Fayard, 1990.

Benjamin, Walter. "Surrealism: The Last Snapshot of the European Intelligentsia." In *One Way Street and Other Writings*, translated by Edmund Jephcott and Kingsley Shorter, 225–39. New York: Harcourt Brace, 1978.

———. *Gesammelte Schriften*. Edited by Rolf Tiedemann and Hermann Schweppenhäuser. Frankfurt: Suhrkamp, 1972–89. Vol. 5: *Das Passagen-Werk* edited by Rolf Tiedemann, 1982.

Bergius, Hanne. "The Ambiguous Aesthetic of Dada: Towards a Definition of its Categories." In *Dada: Studies of a Movement*, edited by Richard Sheppard, 26–38. Norfolk: Alpha Academic, 1979.

———. "dada machinel." In *Kunst und Technik in den 20er Jahren: Neue Sachlichkeit und Gegenständlicher Konstructivismus*. 2 July-10 August 1980, pp. 124–35. München: Städtische Galerie im Lenbachhaus.

Bernheimer, C. *Figures of Ill Repute: Representing Prostitutes in Nineteenth-Century France*. Cambridge: Harvard University Press, 1989.

Bowlt, John E. "Dada in Russia." In *Dada/Dimensions*, edited by Stephen Foster, 221–48. Ann Arbor: UMI Research Press, 1985.

Breton, André. *Manifestos of Surrealism*. Translated by Richard Seaver and Helen R. Lane. Ann Arbor: The University of Michigan Press, 1972.

Brinton, Charles. "Evolution not Revolution in Art," *International Studio* 49 (April 1913): 27–35.

Brown, Milton W. *The Story of the Armory Show*. New York: Abbeville Press and the Joseph Hirshhorn Foundation, 1988.

Browning, Robert. *The Ring and the Book*, with an introduction by Wylie Sypher. New York: Norton, 1961.

———, and Elizabeth Barrett. *The Letters of Robert Browning and Elizabeth Barrett, 1945–1846*. New York: Harper, 1899.

Bruner, Jerome. *Acts of Meaning*. Cambridge: Harvard University Press, 1990.

Bryson, Norman. *Vision and Painting: The Logic of the Gaze*. New Haven: Yale University Press, 1983.

Buchloh, Benjamin H. D. "Allegorical Procedures: Appropriation and Montage in Contemporary Art." *Artforum* 21.1 (September 1982): 43–56.

———. "Figures of Authority, Ciphers of Regression: Notes on the Return of Representation in European Painting." *October* 16 (spring 1981): 39–68.

Bürger, Peter. *The Theory of the Avant-Garde*. Translated by Michael Shaw. Minneapolis: University of Minnesota Press, 1984.

Burke, Carolyn. "Getting Spliced: Modernism and Sexual Difference." *American Quarterly* 39.1 (spring 1987): 98–121.

Chave, Anna C. "New Encounters with *Les Demoiselles d'Avignon*: Gender, Race, and the Origins of Cubism." *The Art Bulletin* 76 (December 1994): 596–611.

Clifford, James. *The Predicament of Culture*. Cambridge: Harvard University Press, 1988.

Coffman, Stanley. *Imagism: A Chapter of the History of Modern Poetry*. Norman: University of Oklahoma Press, 1951.

Costello, Bonnie. *Marianne Moore: Imaginary Possessions*. Cambridge: Harvard University, 1981.

———. "Marianne Moore and the American Sublime." *Sagatrieb* 6.3 (winter 1987): 5–13.

Dachy, Marc. *Dada: The Dada Movement, 1915–1923*. New York: Rizzoli, 1990.

Dech, Gertrud Jula. *Schnitt mit dem Küchenmesser DADA durch die letzte weimarer Bierbauchkulturepoche Deutschlands: Untersuchungen zur Fotomontage bei Hannah Höch*. Munster: Lit. Verlag, 1981.

Derrida, Jacques. *The Truth in Painting*. Translated by Geoff Bennington and Ian McLeod. Chicago: University of Chicago Press, 1987.

DeZayas, Marius. "Pablo Picasso." *Camera Work* 34–35 (April-July 1911): 65–67.

Diehl, Joanne Feit. *Women Poets and the American Sublime*. Bloomington: Indiana University Press, 1990.

Dijkstra, Bram. *Cubism, Stieglitz, and the Early Poetry of William Carlos Williams: The Hieroglyphics of a New Speech*. Princeton: Princeton University Press, 1969.

Drucker, Johanna. "Dada Collage and Photomontage." *Art Journal* 52 (winter 1993): 82–84, 87.

DuPlessis, Rachel Blau. "'Corpses of Poesy': Some Modern Poets and Some Gender Ideologies of Lyric." In *Feminist Measures: Soundings in Poetry and Theory* edited by Lynn Keller and Cristanne Miller, 69–95. Ann Arbor: University of Michigan Press, 1994.

Durham, Carolyn A. "Linguistic and Sexual Engendering in Marianne Moore's Poetry." In *Engendering the Word: Feminist Essays in Psychosexual Poetics,* edited by Temma F. Berg. 224–43. Urbana: University of Illinois Press, 1989.

Erickson, Darlene Williams. *Illusion Is More Precise than Precision: The Poetry of Marianne Moore*. Tuscaloosa: University of Alabama Press, 1992.

Erkkila, Betsy. *The Wicked Sisters: Women Poets, Literary History and Discord*. Oxford: Oxford University Press, 1992.

Eysteinsson, Astradur. *The Concept of Modernism*. Ithaca: Cornell University Press, 1990.

Foucault, Michel. *The Order of Things: An Archaeology of the Human Sciences*. New York: Vintage, 1973.

Fraser, Nancy. "The Uses and Abuses of French Discourse Theory." In *Revaluing French Feminism: Critical Essays on Difference, Agency, & Culture,* edited by Nancy Fraser and Sandra Lee Bartky, 177–94. Bloomington: Indiana University Press, 1992.

Fried, Michael. *Realism, Writing, Disfiguration*. Chicago: University of Chicago Press, 1987.

Fry, Edward F., ed. *Cubism*. New York: McGraw-Hill, 1966.

Geertz, Clifford. *The Interpretation of Culture*. New York: Basic Books, 1973.

Gilbert, Sandra. "Marianne Moore as Female Female Impersonator." In *Marianne Moore: The Art of a Modernist*, edited by Joseph Parisi, 27–46. Ann Arbor: University of Michigan Press, 1990.

———, and Susan Gubar. *Mad Woman in the Attic*. New Haven: Yale University Press, 1980.

Gilmore, Leigh. "The Gaze of the Other Woman: Beholding and Begetting in Dickinson, Moore, and Rich." In *Engendering the Word: Feminist Essays in Psychosexual Poetics,* edited by Temma F. Berg, 81–102. Urbana: University of Illinois Press, 1989.

Godwin, William. *Enquiry Concerning Political Justice and Its Influence on Morals and Happiness*. Edited by F. E. L. Priestley. Toronto: University of Toronto Press, 1946.

Goodman, Nelson. *Languages of Art*. New York: Bobbs-Merrill, 1968.

Goulding, John. *Cubism: A History and an Analysis, 1907–1914*. London: Faber and Faber, 1988.

Green, Martin. *New York 1913: The Armory Show and the Paterson Strike Pageant*. New York: Scribners, 1988.

Greenberg, Clement. "Collage." In *Collage: Critical Views,* edited by Katherine Hoffman, 67–77. Ann Arbor: UMI Research Press, 1989.

Gregory, Elizabeth. *Quotation and Modern American Poetry: "Imaginary Gardens with Real Toads."* Houston: Rice University Press, 1996.

Guilbaut, Serge. *How New York Stole the Idea of Modern Art: Abstract Expressionism, Freedom and the Cold War*. Translated by Arthur Goldhammer. Chicago: University of Chicago Press, 1983.

Guillory, Daniel L. "Marianne Moore and Technology." In *Marianne Moore: Woman and Poet,* edited by Patricia C. Willis, 83–91. Orono: National Poetry Foundation, University of Maine, 1990.

Hadas, Pamela White. *Marianne Moore: Poet of Affection*. Syracuse, N.Y.: Syracuse University Press, 1977.

Hall, Donald. *Marianne Moore: The Cage and the Animal*. New York: Pegasus, 1970.

Hancock, Jane. "Arp's Chance Collages." In *Dada/Dimensions,* edited by Stephen C. Foster, 47–82. Ann Arbor, Mich.: UMI Research Press, 1985.

Hazlitt, William. "On the Prose Style of Poets." In *The Complete Works of William Hazlitt,* edited by P. P. Howe, 5–16. London: Dent, 1930–34.

Heuving, Jeanne. *Gender in the Art of Marianne Moore: Omissions Are Not Accidents*. Detroit: Wayne State University Press, 1992.

Hogue, Cynthia. *Scheming Women: Poetry, Privilege and the Politics of Subjectivity.* Albany: SUNY Press, 1995.

Holley, Margaret. *The Poetry of Marianne Moore: A Study in Voice and Value.* Cambridge: Cambridge University Press, 1987.

Jefferson, Ann. "Literariness, Dominance and Violence in Formalist Aesthetics." In *Literary Theory Today,* edited by Peter Collier and Helga Geyer-Ryan, 125–41. Ithaca: Cornell University Press, 1990.

Johnson, Clifton. *What to See in America.* New York: Macmillan, 1919.

Keller, Lynn. "'For inferior who is free?' Liberating the Woman Writer in Marianne Moore's 'Marriage.'" In *Influence and Intertextuality in Literary History,* edited by Jay Clayton and Eric Rothstein, 219–44. Madison: University of Wisconsin Press, 1991.

———, and Christanne Miller. "'The Tooth of Disputation': Marianne Moore's 'Marriage.'" *Sagetreib* 6.3 (winter 1987): 99–116.

Kenner, Hugh. *A Homemade World: The American Modernist Writers.* New York: Alfred A. Knopf, 1975.

Korg, Jacob. "The Dialogic Nature of Collage in Pound's *Cantos.*" *Mosaic* 22.2 (spring 1989): 95–109.

Kristeva, Julia. *Revolution in Poetic Language.* Translated by Margaret Waller. New York: Columbia University Press, 1984.

Lavin, Maud. *Cut with the Kitchen Knife: The Weimar Photomontages of Hannah Höch.* New Haven: Yale University Press, 1993.

Leavell, Linda. *Marianne Moore and the Visual Arts: Prismatic Color.* Baton Rouge: Louisiana State University Press, 1995.

Leighton, Patricia. "'La Propagande par le Rire': Satire's Subversion in Apollinaire, Jarry and Picasso's Collages." *Gazette de Beaux Arts* 12 (October 1988): 163–70.

Lippard, Lucy, ed. *Dadas on Art.* Englewood Cliffs, N.J.: Prentice-Hall, 1971.

Littell, Philip. Review of George Santayana's poetry. *The New Republic* 34.433 (21 March 1923): 102.

Martin, Taffy. *Marianne Moore: Subversive Modernist.* Austin: University of Texas Press, 1986.

Mathews, Tim. "The Machine: Dada, Vorticism and the Future." In *The Violent Muse: Violence and the Artistic Imagination in Europe, 1910–1939,* edited by Jana Howlett and Rod Mengham, 124–40. Manchester: Manchester University Press, 1994.

McCole, John. *Walter Benjamin and the Antinomies of Tradition.* Ithaca: Cornell University Press, 1993.

Melzer, Annabelle. *Dada and Surrealist Performance.* Baltimore: The Johns Hopkins University Press, 1994.

Merrin, Judith. *An Enabling Humility: Marianne Moore, Elizabeth Bishop, and the Uses of Tradition.* New Brunswick, N.J.: Rutgers University Press, 1990.

Miller, Cristanne. *Marianne Moore: Questions of Authority.* Cambridge: Harvard University Press, 1995.

Milman, Estera. "Dada New York: An Historiographic Analysis." In *Dada/Dimensions,* edited by Stephen Foster, 165–86. Ann Arbor, Mich.: UMI Research Press, 1985.

Mitchell, W. J. T. *Iconology: Image, Text, Ideology.* Chicago: University of Chicago Press, 1986.

Molesworth, Charles. *Marianne Moore: A Literary Life.* New York: Atheneum, 1990.

Moore, Marianne. *The Complete Prose.* Edited by Patricia Willis. New York: Viking, 1987.

———. *The Complete Poems of Marianne Moore.* New York: Macmillan, 1967.

———. *Observations*. New York: The Dial Press, 1924.
———. "Concerning the Marvelous." Archives of American Art 2166, Column 523, Alfred Barr papers.
Mulvey, Laura. "Visual Pleasure and Narrative Cinema." *Screen* 16.3 (autumn 1975): 6–18.
Natural Parks Portfolio, The. Department of the Interior Rules and Regulations, 1922. Rosenbach Museum and Library.
Naumann, Francis M. *New York Dada, 1915–1923*. New York: Abrams, 1994.
Pach, Walter. "The Cubist Room." In vol. 2, *Pamphlets*, of *The Armory Show: International Exhibition of Modern Art, 1913*. New York: Arno Press, 1972.
Paterson, Lee. "Literary History." In *Critical Terms for Literary Study*, 2nd ed., edited by Frank Lentricchia and Thomas McLaughlin, 250–62. Chicago: University of Chicago Press, 1995.
Perloff, Marjorie. "The Invention of Collage." In *Collage,* edited by Jeannine Parisier Plottel, 5–47. New York: New York Literary Forum, 1983.
Poggi, Christine. *In Defiance of Painting: Cubism, Futurism and the Invention of Collage*. New Haven: Yale University Press, 1992.
Reade, Charles. *Christie Johnstone*. [1885]. Paris: The Grolier Society, n.d.
Ricoeur, Paul. *Freud and Philosophy: An Essay on Interpretation*. Translated by Denis Savage. New Haven: Yale University Press, 1970.
Rihbany, Abraham Mitram. *The Syrian Christ*. Boston: Houghton Mifflin, 1916.
Roditi, Edouard. "Interview with Hannah Höch." *Arts* 34.3 (December 1959): 24–29.
Roosevelt, Theodore. "A Layman's Views of an Art Exhibition." *Outlook* 103 (29 March 1913): 718–20.
Rubin, William. "Picasso and Braque: An Introduction." In *Picasso and Braque: Pioneering Cubism,* 15–62. New York: Museum of Modern Art, 1989.
Sahlins, Marshall. *How "natives" think: about Captain Cook, for example*. Chicago: University of Chicago Press, 1995.
Sanders, Emmy Veronica. "America Invades Europe. *Broom* 1 (November 1921): 90–91.
Schulman, Grace. *Marianne Moore: The Poetry of Engagement*. Urbana: University of Illinois Press, 1986.
Schulte-Sasse, Jochen. Introduction to *Theory of the Avant Garde*. Edited by Peter Bürger. Translated by Michael Shaw. Minneapolis: University of Minnesota Press, 1984.
Schulze, Robin Gail. *The Web of Friendship: Marianne Moore and Wallace Stevens*. Ann Arbor: University of Michigan Press, 1995.
———. "'The Frigate Pelican''s Progress: Marianne Moore's Multiple Versions and Modernist Practice." In *Gendered Modernisms: American Women Poets and Their Readers,* edited by Margaret Dickie and Thomas Travisano, 117–39. Philadelphia: University of Pennsylvania Press, 1996.
Slatin, John Meyer. *"The Savage's Romance": The Poetry of Marianne Moore*. University Park: Pennsylvania State University Press, 1986.
Stanlis, Peter J., ed. *Edmund Burke: Selected Writings and Speeches*. Gloucester, Mass.: Peter Smith, 1968.
Stapleton, Laurence. *Marianne Moore: The Poet's Advance*. Princeton: Princeton University Press, 1978.
Staten, Henry. *Wittgenstein and Derrida*. Lincoln: University of Nebraska Press, 1984.
Stein, Gertrude. *Matisse, Picasso and Gertrude Stein with two shorter stories*. Millerton, N.Y.: Something Else Press, 1972.
———. "Picasso." *Camera Work* special number (August 1912): 29–30.

Steinberg, Leo. "The Philosophical Brothel." *October* 44 (spring 1988): 3–74.

Steiner, Wendy. *The Colors of Rhetoric: Problems in the Relation between Modern Literature and Painting*. Chicago: University of Chicago Press, 1982.

———. *Exact Resemblance to Exact Resemblance: The Literary Portraiture of Gertrude Stein*. New Haven: Yale University Press, 1978.

Steinman, Lisa M. "'So As to Be One Having Some Way of Being One Having Some Way of Working': Marianne Moore and Literary Tradition." In *Gendered Modernisms: American Women Poets and Their Readers,* edited by Margaret Dickie and Thomas Travisano, 97–116. Philadelphia: University of Pennsylvania Press, 1996,

Sypher, Wylie. Introduction to *The Ring and the Book* by Robert Borwning. New York: Norton, 1961.

Tashjian, Dickran. *Joseph Cornell: Gifts of Desire*. Miami Beach, Fla.: Grassfield Press, 1992.

Thomas, Edward. *Feminine Influence on the Poets*. London: Martin Secker, 1910.

Torgovnik, Marianna. Introduction to *The Visual Arts, Pictorialism and the Novel: James, Lawrence and Woolf.* Princeton: Princeton University Press, 1985.

Trollope, Anthony. *Barchester Towers*. Vol. 2. New York: Dodd, Mead, 1904.

Tzara, Tristan. *Seven Dada Manifestos and Lampisteries*. Translated by Barbara Wright. New York: Riverrun, 1977.

Varnedoe, Kirk. *A Fine Disregard*. New York: Museum of Modern Art, 1990.

Walton, Kendall. *Mimesis as Makebelieve: On the Foundations of the Representational Arts*. Cambridge: Harvard University Press, 1990.

Ward, Francis. "'Poison-Gas' in Nature: The Lesser Octopus." *Illustrated London News* 163 (11 August 1923): 270.

Wheeler, Monroe. "Reminiscence." In *Festschrift for Marianne Moore's Seventy-seventh Birthday by Various Hands* (New York: Tambimuttu and Mass, 1964), 127–30.

Wilcox, W. D. *The Rockies of Canada*. New York: Putnam, 1903.

Williams, William Carlos. *Selected Letters*. Edited by John Thirwall. New York: McDowell, Oblensky, 1984.

Willis, Patricia. "The Road to Paradise: First Notes on 'An Octopus'." *Twentieth Century Literature* 30 (summer/fall 1984): 242–66.

Yeats, William Butler. *Ideas of Good and Evil*. New York: Russell and Russell, 1967.

Index